Deciphering the Holy Ghost

UNDERSTANDING THE SPIRIT OF THE LORD, ITS MANIFESTATIONS AND WORKS

DAVID MURESAN
LIGHT FOR GOD MINISTRY
LIGHTFORGOD.COM

Table of Contents

Introduction 7

Part 1: Seven-Fold Spirit...14

    The Spirit of Fear of the Lord 14

    The Spirit of Wisdom 17

    The Spirit of Knowledge..19

    The Spirit of Understanding....................................22

    The Spirit of Counsel...25

    The Spirit of Might 29

    The Spirit of the Lord 33

Part 2: Seven Eyes of the Seven Spirits 38

    The First Eye (Eyes) 45

    The Second Eye (Ears) 47

    The Third Eye (Mouth)..50

    The Fourth Eye (Mind and Thoughts) 53

    The Fifth Eye (Heart)...54

    The Sixth Eye (Feet) 56

    The Seventh Eye (Hands) 58

Part 3: Symbols of the Holy Spirit...............................67

Part 4: Receiving, Filling & Baptism in the Holy Spirit 85

    Receiving..86

    Being Filled 88

    Baptism in Holy Spirit 90

    Baptism of Fire 94

Part 5: Nine Gifts of the Holy Spirit 105

Wisdom and Knowledge...106

Gift of Faith 109

Gift of Healing...113

Gift of Miracles..117

Gift of Prophecy 121

Discerning of Spirits 126

Different kinds of Tongues 131

Interpretation of Tongues..134

Part 6: Ministry of the Holy Spirit 143

Part 7: Rejecting the Holy Spirit..201

Lying to the Holy Spirit 201

Grieving the Holy Spirit 203

Quenching the Holy Spirit 204

Resisting the Holy Spirit...206

Blasphemy against the Holy Spirit 207

Introduction

The purpose of this book is to be able to put together and decipher the Holy Spirit and be able to comprehend who He is and what He does. I decided to write this book for the purpose of filling a gap in today's world and teachings. I have looked in many places and have seen many books about the Holy Spirit, but not one of them was the whole picture of the Holy Ghost. He is either spoken about in one way or another. Either people relate to Him as a symbol of fire, as a dove or as water, but in the Word of God we learn about many more symbols of the Holy Spirit, which will be covered in Part 3 of this book.

I have talked to, and asked, many Christians about the Holy Spirit and I ask them, "What does the Holy Spirit do?" They respond back by saying that the Holy Spirit will convict the world of sin, that we are sealed with Him for life if we have accepted Christ, and that He will give us power. Which is good and all, but if you ask them what else they know, they say that is all. They do not know anything else because they were not taught or did not study the Word of God for themselves.

This is the second purpose of this book: to fill the gap, the void, of knowledge about the Holy Spirit that the children of God have in today's generation.

Furthermore, this book took shape because I realized that this gap of knowledge in the world has also made many of us lost and confused about who the Holy Ghost is and what He can do. This is very heartbreaking, especially when we call ourselves children of God. We must study the Word of God and see fully why He has given this gift to us and why we need Him every moment of everyday. Jesus Christ Himself said, "I must go so that the Holy Ghost can come." This indicates that the Holy Spirit has a great purpose that He must fulfill in us and through us. We must be aware of this so that we can unlock this potential and allow the Holy Spirit to work to the fullest extent in His mission for our lives and around us.

A last reason for this book is to inform you and help you realize that we can do things that go against the Holy Spirit Himself and His mission. We need to understand this and not hinder His work. Take this to heart, so we can fulfil God's will with the Spirit of God that He has sealed us with.

I pray that this book will counsel you in the right way, to understand what God has in store for you, so you can gain knowledge, wisdom, and might in His word. I pray that this book will put the Fear of the Lord in you so that you will be able to gain His wisdom and knowledge. I pray that throughout reading this book that the Spirit of the Lord will be upon you and that He will give you more light, to open your eyes to the truth and what God has done for you through His Spirit.

I would like to end by saying that, before reading, ask God to work in your heart while reading this book, allow His anointment to be upon you, to truly understand my words. Ask God to open your heart to the truth and be able to accept it even if it is, maybe, against what you have been taught until now or have thought was true. To accept God's will, we must have an open heart to understand and to listen, otherwise we will hinder ourselves from understanding because we do not like it or because of our hardened heart of disbelief.

God's truth is not man's truth. God's understanding is not man's understanding and His commands are His alone. Do not close yourself off to the power of God because you don't understand it or are afraid of it, like many do today, and because of this they say it isn't God at work. For God's power is true and real and beyond what any one of us can fully understand.

I would like to let you know that the format of this book may be a little different than others you have read in the past. It includes many verses from the Bible for each subject, but it should be quite easy to follow and understand.

God Bless you.

The Holy Spirit

The Holy Spirit is a topic that is diversely spoken about and has many teachings about it throughout different denominations. It is also known as the Spirit of God or the Holy Ghost, among many other names. I would like us to go into the Bible and see what the Word of God says about the Spirit of God, why we need Him, and why He was sent to us, as well as His manifestation, gifts, responsibilities, and signs. Once we

8

understand all those, we will have further insight into who God is and His Spirit.

To start off, we need to understand that the Holy Spirit is seven spirits in one, one Spirit within a seven-fold (essence), just as the Father, Son, and Holy Ghost are one, a three-fold (essence) of God. These Spirits are the Spirit of Wisdom, Spirit of Knowledge, Spirit of Understanding, Spirit of Counsel, Spirit of Might, Spirit of Fear, and lastly, the Spirit of the Lord, written about in Isaiah 11:2 and Revelation 1:4, 4:5, and 5:6.

Additionally, the Holy Spirit also carries nine gifts that may manifest through a baptized believer. These Gifts are Wisdom, Knowledge, Faith, Healing, Miracles, Prophecy, Discerning of Spirits, Diverse Tongues, and Interpretation of Tongues. Likewise, the Holy Spirit has symbols/signs that the Word of God uses to resemble the Holy Spirit. These are the symbols of a Dove, Oil (anointed), Water, Breath/Wind, Cloud, Rain, River, Dew, Wine, Clothing, Finger, Hand, Seal, Fire, and Gift.

There are also other ways that The Spirt of the Lord can manifest in the believer, other than the specific nine Gifts mentioned above. For example, some may have dreams, others visions, and still others may have revelations that are given to them.

We also need to recognize that those with the Holy Spirit will have what the Word of God calls 'Fruits,' which we should have in our lives by living in the Spirit as a new creation and the Spirit living in us, in our Lord Jesus Christ. These gifts are written in Galatians 5:16-26. The Holy Spirit is also given to us as a Power, a Comforter, Helper, Guider, Testifier, Sanctifier,

9

Revealer, Advocate, as Hope, for Prayer, Conviction, Remembrance, for Evangelism, and for leading us to Truth, along with many other things which we will all cover. On top of this, we will also cover ways we can grieve the Spirit or go against the Spirit of God.

Before we go further on, here are some names given to the Lord's Spirit (not including symbols):

1. Holy Spirit
2. Holy Ghost
3. Spirit of the Lord
4. Spirit of God
5. Seven Spirits of Wisdom, Knowledge, Understanding, Counsel, Might, Fear, and Spirit of Lord
6. Oil (anointment) and the rest of the Symbol/Signs

Part 1:
Seven-Fold Spirit

Let's go into the Seven Spirits of God to determine what they are used for and what they accomplish in us and through us.

The Spirit of Fear of the Lord

- Deuteronomy 10:12 – And now, Israel, what doth the LORD thy God require of thee, but to fear the LORD thy God, to walk in all his ways, and to love him, and to serve the LORD thy God with all thy heart and with all thy soul...
- Psalms 25:12 – What man is he that feareth the LORD? Him shall he teach in the way that he shall choose.
- Psalms 25:14 – The secret of the LORD is with them that fear him; and he will shew them his covenant.
- Proverbs 2:1-5 – My son, if thou wilt receive my words, and hide my commandments with thee; So that thou incline thine ear unto wisdom, and apply thine heart to understanding; Yea, if thou criest after knowledge, and liftest up thy voice for understanding; If thou seekest her as silver, and searchest

for her as for hid treasures; Then shalt thou understand the fear of the LORD, and find the knowledge of God.

- Proverbs 9:10 – The fear of the LORD is the beginning of wisdom: and the knowledge of the holy is understanding.
- Proverbs 22:4 – By humility and the fear of the LORD are riches, and honour, and life.
- 2 Corinthians 7:1 – Having therefore these promises, dearly beloved, let us cleanse ourselves from all filthiness of the flesh and spirit, perfecting holiness in the fear of God.
- Revelation 14:7 – Saying with a loud voice, Fear God, and give glory to him; for the hour of his judgment is come: and worship him that made heaven, and earth, and the sea, and the fountains of waters.

I would like to speak about the Spirit of Fear first, since this is the spirit that activates or opens the door to the other spirits: the Spirits of Wisdom, Knowledge, Understanding, and the others can all come through the Spirit of Fear. One of the first things we need to cover is the term "fear;" in Hebrew the word is Yir-'at, this word meaning not just fear but "reverential awe" (glory), respect, and love. If you read these verses with the word "respect" or "reverential awe" instead of fear, the meaning seems to change, but it doesn't change. It just makes it easier for us to understand for our modern time period, as compared to what they understood then.

In 2 Corinthians 7, it is written for us to strive for "perfecting holiness in the fear of God." This fear is the same fear as reverential awe or respect. We must realize that respect is not a feeling, but an action based off of a feeling, meaning the love and respect, that awe, that we have for God, for who He is as the creator of the Heavens and Earth, the creator of you,

13

sitting on an everlasting throne, having no time, omnipresent, omnipotent, all knowing, Alpha and the Omega, and King of Kings (you can read Revelation 14:7). This respect is what keeps you and me growing in Christ. Also, it is what makes us follow Him, just as the apostles followed Him in the gospel. It is the awe of His glory and what He is able to do as the Lord Jesus Christ.

When we look at it this way, this type of fear is a fear that allows us to have access, to look at God as a mentor, someone to learn from, someone to observe, someone to gain experience from including wisdom, knowledge, and understanding. A fear consisting of respect and love is a fear that gives you the opportunity to grow. When the Word of God, which is sharper than a two-edged sword, speaks, it convicts you and it cuts and divides the soul and spirit. Someone that has this fear will listen to the Holy Ghost and grow spiritually for they understand that God has spoken and their awe towards God will lead them to transform themselves in Christ.

Psalms 25:12 says that those that fear Him, He can teach. This is true – if you do not respect someone and love them, you will not accept their teaching. For through your own pride you will assume you know better than they. This will lead you further away from truth, further from Wisdom, Knowledge, Understanding, and Counsel. In Proverbs 25:14, it says that through the Fear of the Lord He will show you His covenant. The word used here means "alliance" in Hebrew; this fear will have access to God's alliance with us, a union that was made so we can both benefit from it. God wants a real relationship with us, a true intimate relation, a partnership that both we and God benefit from. This Fear is the master key to the rest of the six

14

Spirits. It is time to take the master key and use it in our lives so that we can start truly growing in Christ. Take the master key and open the door.

The Spirit of Wisdom

- Exodus 31:3 – And I have filled him with the spirit of God, in wisdom, and in understanding, and in knowledge, and in all manner of workmanship.
- 1 Kings 4:29 – And God gave Solomon wisdom and understanding exceeding much, and largeness of heart, even as the sand that is on the sea shore.
- Job 12:12 – With the ancient *is* wisdom; and in length of days understanding.
- Job 28:28 – And unto man he said, Behold, the fear of the Lord, that *is* wisdom; and to depart from evil *is* understanding.
- Proverbs 1:23 – Turn you at my reproof: behold, I will pour out my spirit unto you, I will make known my words unto you.
- Proverbs 2:6 – For the LORD giveth wisdom: out of his mouth *cometh* knowledge and understanding; …
- Proverbs 3:19 – The LORD by wisdom hath founded the earth; by understanding hath he established the heavens; …
- Proverbs 9:10 – The fear of the LORD *is* the beginning of wisdom: and the knowledge of the holy *is* understanding.

The Spirit of Wisdom is something that many may claim they have but do not. Now, when we think of wisdom, we always think of someone old, someone that has experience and because of this experience we say they are wise, for we can learn from them. If we look at Job, chapter 12, it states that with age/ancient, as stated in KJV, comes wisdom - so even here we can see that, yes, with greater age we get more wisdom. Also, we find in Scripture that the beginning of wisdom is the Fear of the Lord. We need to understand that if we have the proper Fear of the Lord, as in who God is - the creator of all, full of all wisdom and how all has been created, understanding that He is Holy above all - we can start understanding this wisdom.

God can start working in you to give you this wisdom. One thing we need to comprehend is that if God gives us the gift of the Spirit of Wisdom, we can be of any age, 10 or 25 or 30, and men and women will see something different about you. When you have the Spirit of Wisdom, others will say that you, at your age, have wisdom beyond your age. This wisdom will be applicable in the life of even those people older than you by 10 or 30 years. You will have wisdom that others will come for and search out to have their problems and situations resolved. Just as we see in the Word of God that many came to Solomon for this wisdom and to see it for themselves in action.

Another application of wisdom is how God's Word will be known to you, that you will know what God's words will be, for the Spirit will speak through you the wisdom of God. In Proverbs 3, it is written that God created/founded the Earth and established the heavens with wisdom, therefore, part of God's wisdom given to us through the Spirit of the Lord is the ways of how God created the world in the supernatural way. God can give the wisdom of man, meaning the wisdom of what we need down here, the wisdom to flourish, nurture, to have power - everything we consider wisdom down here. Even this does not make you wise - for example Job 32 states that even "great men are not always wise," which means someone may be wise on man's terms, but not in front of God.

On top of this, He can give the supernatural wisdom of Himself and His creation of the world and the universe, of how things came to be. God's wisdom, simply put, is what we consider the supernatural/mystical – intelligence/intellect of God's thinking, justness, creation, power, and the supremacy of His authority overall. Things that seem hidden or kept secret from us, or what we consider the mystery of God (we hear people always say that God works in mysterious ways), shall be open to us and revealed to us, through the Spirit of Wisdom and Understanding. If you want to start understanding how God truly works and the wisdom He has, it is time for us to make an effort and start asking to receive this wisdom, to understand and give Him glory for who He is.

The Spirit of Knowledge

- Genesis 2:9 – And out of the ground made the LORD God to grow every tree that is pleasant to the sight, and good for food; the tree of life also in the midst of the garden, and the tree of knowledge of good and evil.
- 1 Kings 3:9 – "So give Your servant an understanding heart to judge Your people to discern between good and evil. For who is able to judge this great people of Yours?"
- Psalms 69:5 – O God, it is You who knows my folly, And my wrongs are not hidden from You.
- Psalms 119:66 – Teach me good discernment and knowledge, For I believe in Your commandments.
- Proverbs 1:4 – To give subtilty to the simple, To the young knowledge and discretion…
- Proverbs 1:7 – The fear of the LORD is the beginning of knowledge; Fools despise wisdom and instruction.

- Proverbs 2:3-5 – For if you cry for discernment, Lift your voice for understanding; If you seek her as silver And search for her as for hidden treasures; Then you will discern the fear of the LORD And discover the knowledge of God.
- Proverbs 12:1 – Whoever loves discipline loves knowledge, but he who hates reproof is stupid.
- Proverbs 18:15 – The mind of the prudent acquires knowledge, And the ear of the wise seeks knowledge.
- Hosea 6:6 – For I delight in loyalty rather than sacrifice, and in the knowledge of God rather than burnt offerings.
- Luke 17: 11 – But He knew their thoughts and said to them, "Any kingdom divided against itself is laid waste; and a house divided against itself falls.
- 1 Corinthians 12:8 – For to one is given the word of wisdom through the Spirit, and to another the word of knowledge according to the same Spirit…
- 1 John 3:20 – in whatever our heart condemns us; for God is greater than our heart and knows all things.
- 1 John 3:24 – The one who keeps His commandments abides in Him, and He in him We know by this that He abides in us, by the Spirit whom He has given us.
- 2 Peter 1:2-5 – Grace and peace be multiplied unto you through the knowledge of God, and of Jesus our Lord, According as his divine power hath given unto us all things that pertain unto life and godliness, through the knowledge of him that hath called us to glory and virtue: Whereby are given unto us exceeding great and precious promises: that by these ye might be partakers of the divine nature, having escaped the corruption that is in the world through lust. And beside this, giving all diligence, add to your faith virtue; and to virtue knowledge; …

The Spirit of Knowledge is a different Spirit and Gift than the Spirit of Wisdom. Proverbs 18 writes that the wise will seek knowledge, meaning that you can be wise but still need to seek knowledge. This means you might meet people that are wise, but they also seem that they have no knowledge. I know this is hard to understand. Most of the time these are given together, but not always. I have met many people in the past that seemed very knowledgeable but were not wise at all. I have also met many people that are wise but do not have knowledge about what they are wise about.

As we have seen before, wisdom is God's supernatural intellect or what we call His mysteries. These mysteries are how God puts things together, how they function; if you remember, above was written about how God created the earth and heavens through wisdom. On the other hand, the Spirit of Knowledge is knowing what is good and evil, knowing wrong from right, and how to apply the wisdom you have, as the Word of the God states in Genesis 2. Also, in 1 Kings 3, God gives Solomon Understanding and Knowledge to be able to discern good from evil for the nation of God, to be able to apply judgment properly. We also see that in Proverbs 12, it talks about that whoever loves discipline loves knowledge, meaning that by loving discipline (discipleship) you can reach knowledge. To be able to understand what is good and evil requires discipline.

In 2 Peter, it is written that by divine power God has given life and godliness through knowledge. This means that through this divine power (Spirit of Knowledge) we have access to choose life and what leads us to godliness. Godliness is to conform to what God wants, His laws, what is righteous, what is holy and good in front of God, to become more like Christ. The

Spirit of Knowledge will direct us into what God desires, how to be Holy, to know what is right from wrong and to discern good and evil and follow Him with our full heart, spirit, soul, and body. When we do this, we will be able to live a pleasing life to God, a holy, and Spirit-filled life.

As children of God we should search for the Spirit of Knowledge, as it says in Proverbs 2, as for hidden treasure and with the Fear of the Lord, which is another Spirit of the Lord, and through this we will discover the Knowledge of God. Anyone that has truth and knowledge of discernment will always choose in the end what brings life over death, if they stay strong in their ways without wavering. If you have been struggling in your life about what is good in front of God's eyes, and not man's, it is time to start asking to receive knowledge about what you are struggling with so you will be able to start discerning what is good in front of God. Many times, we mess up in our lives because we ask for wisdom when we need knowledge or we ask for knowledge when we need wisdom; we need to know the difference for us to understand what we need to ask for and receive what we need. That is why it says that when you don't know what to pray for, the Holy Spirit prays.

The Spirit of Understanding

- Job 28:28 – And unto man he said, Behold, the fear of the LORD, that is wisdom; and to depart from evil is understanding.
- Psalms 119:27 – Make me to understand the way of thy precepts: so shall I talk of thy wondrous works.
- Psalms 119:130 – The entrance of thy words giveth light; it giveth understanding unto the simple.

- Proverbs 2:2-5 – So that thou incline thine ear unto wisdom, and apply thine heart to understanding; Yea, if thou criest after knowledge, and liftest up thy voice for understanding; If thou seekest her as silver, and searchest for her as for hid treasures; Then shalt thou understand the fear of the LORD, and find the knowledge of God.
- Proverbs 2:11-15 – Discretion shall preserve thee, understanding shall keep thee: To deliver thee from the way of the evil man, from the man that speaketh froward things; Who leave the paths of uprightness, to walk in the ways of darkness; Who rejoice to do evil, and delight in the frowardess of the wicked; Whose ways are crooked, and they froward in their paths: ...
- Proverbs 3:5 – Trust in the LORD with all your heart, and do not lean on your own understanding.
- Proverbs 3:7 – Wisdom is the principal thing; therefore, get wisdom: and with all thy getting get understanding.
- Proverbs 14:29 – He that is slow to wrath is of great understanding: but he that is hasty of spirit exalteth folly.
- Proverbs 17:27 – He that hath knowledge spareth his words: and a man of understanding is of an excellent (calm) spirit.
- Proverbs 20:5 – Counsel in the heart of man is like deep water; but a man of understanding will draw it out.
- Proverbs 24:3-4 – Through wisdom is an house builded; and by understanding it is established: And by knowledge shall the chambers be filled with all precious and pleasant riches.
- Daniel 5:14 – I have even heard of thee, that the spirit of the gods is in thee, and that light and understanding and excellent wisdom is found in thee.
- Hosea 4:14 – I will not punish your daughters when they commit whoredom, nor your spouses when they commit

21

adultery: for themselves are separated with whores, and they sacrifice with harlots: therefore the people that doth not understand shall fall.

- Luke 24:45 – Then opened he their understanding, that they might understand the scriptures…

We need to comprehend that the Spirit of Understanding is different than the Spirit of Knowledge and Wisdom. In Job, it says that Fear of the Lord is Wisdom and we know that the Spirit of Knowledge reveals what is good and evil, what is pure and what is not. In Job, it also says that to DEPART from evil is Understanding, meaning that knowledge is what opens you to good and evil and Understanding is what departs you from that evil. In Psalms 119:27, it is written, "make me understand thy precepts," which are principles, values, morality, and ethics. Which means that if we understand this, it will help us depart from evil for when we understand and see God's ethic, His morals, His values, and His precepts, we will have insight of how God sees and how He feels about sin, transgression, and iniquity, and what is wrong, impure, and unrighteous.

Psalms 119:130 states that the entrance/unfolding of God's Word imparts onto us understanding. This is also the Spirit that Daniel had in Daniel 5:14, for him to be able to understand dreams, a way of interpretation. The Spirit of understanding is what makes us understand dreams and visions that the Holy Spirit gives the children of God, as we see in Daniel. Here we need to understand that when the Holy Spirit manifests His power through us and gives us dreams and visions of things to come, or reveals to us what some call revelations, we must also ask Him to give us the meaning, the understanding, of that dream or vision. Also, the Spirit of Understanding does not

22

just preserve us, but it keeps us from evil and the way of evil men, which Proverbs 2 writes about. Proverbs 14 and 17 speak about the Spirit of Understanding being slow to wrath/anger and having an excellent, still, and unshakable spirit. This means that it will keep us from going into wrath and into recklessness and becoming unstable in our lives or in the problems that we consistently encounter in our daily walk.

In Proverbs 20 it writes that counsel in a man's heart is like deep water, unknown, but someone with understanding will bring it out into the light. In Proverbs 24:3, it's written that through wisdom a house is built but by understanding it is established. Think of wisdom as being a material, meaning you know with this material you can build a house and it exists. Establishing it is understanding, meaning how to keep it together over a long period of time. With wisdom it was built but without proper understanding of how to maintain it, it will fall apart, whether home, life, marriage, career, or your business.

In short, The Spirit of Understanding is putting everything together; it's the illumination of God's Word, the Wisdom and Knowledge He has given us. Without this understanding, just as it says in Hosea 4, all shall fall. Understanding is the vital key of God's Wisdom, Knowledge, and Counsel and the rest of the Spirits.

The Spirit of Counsel

- 1 Kings 12:7 – And they spake unto him, saying, If thou wilt be a servant unto this people this day, and wilt serve them, and answer them, and speak good words to them, then they will be thy servants for ever.

- Psalms 32:8 – I will instruct thee and teach thee in the way which thou shalt go: I will guide thee with mine eye.
- Psalms 73:24 – Thou shalt guide me with thy counsel, and afterward receive me to glory.
- Proverbs 9:9 – Give instruction (Counsel) to a wise man, and he will be yet wiser: teach a just man, and he will increase in learning.
- Proverbs 11:14 – Where no counsel is, the people fall: but in the multitude of counsellors there is safety.
- Proverbs 12:15 – The way of a fool is right in his own eyes: but he that hearkeneth unto counsel is wise.
- Proverbs 13:20 – He that walketh with wise men shall be wise: but a companion of fools shall be destroyed.
- Proverbs 15:22 – Without counsel purposes are disappointed: but in the multitude of counsellors they are established.
- Proverbs 19:20-21- Hear counsel, and receive instruction, that thou mayest be wise in thy latter end. There are many devices in a man's heart; nevertheless the counsel of the LORD, that shall stand.
- Proverbs 20:18 – Every purpose is established by counsel: and with good advice make war.
- Jerimiah 38:15 – Then Jeremiah said unto Zedekiah, If I declare it unto thee, wilt thou not surely put me to death? And if I give thee counsel, wilt thou not hearken unto me?
- John 16:13 – Howbeit when he, the Spirit of (shows the) truth, is come, he will guide you into all truth: for he shall not speak of himself; but whatsoever he shall hear, that shall he speak: and he will shew you things to come.

- Ephesian 1:11 – In whom also we have obtained an inheritance, being predestinated according to the purpose of him who worketh all things after the counsel of his own will...

The Spirit of Counsel is another very important Spirit. I would say out of the five so far spoken about, but even out of the seven, the Spirit of Counsel is one of the few that many children of God encounter more of or understand. When we think about counsel we always think about counseling or a style of therapy. This Spirit of Counsel is not just to help us, but also for advice, support, assistance, instruction, and guidance. In Psalms 32:8, it is written, "I will instruct and teach you in the way you should go." In Psalms 73:24, it is written, "You should guide me, through Your counsel." Just these few verses show us that God, through the Spirit of Counsel, will teach us, instruct us, and guide us in the ways we should go.

When we are in a situation in life, and we are confused, and do not know the way we should go, the Spirit of Counsel will show and guide us in the way we should go. The reason I say that the children of God are most familiar with the Spirit of Counsel is because one of the most common phrases you hear God's children use is, "I felt a presence," or "I heard a voice," or, "I was guided in this direction." This guidance, this voice, came from the Spirit of Counsel, doing His job, trying to let you know which direction you should go in. One perspective we need to see is that when the Spirit of God may speak to you, or try to teach you or guide you or give you advice, counsel you in the proper direction (towards truth), this truth or direction is the will of God for you and me.

We need to understand that we have the choice to listen and follow; 1 Kings 12:7, shows that advice was given for a direction to take, saying if you do this, they will be your servants forever. Proverbs 19:20 says, hear counsel. In Jerimiah 38:15 it says if I give you counsel, will you hear? These are stating that He can show you through counsel, through advice, the way you should go, but will you hear it, will you take the guidance the counselor has given to you? This is very important - if we don't pay attention to advice or guidance, we become numb to it, we become 'above' the advice.

What I mean is that if you stop listening to what the Spirit of Counsel speaks to you or guides you into, eventually you will become numb to it and will no longer hear His voice or see His guidance in your life. The reason this happens is because we forget how His guidance is given, we forget how He speaks and what His voice sounds like. We can see in Proverbs 11:14, it says that without counsel people fail, but where there are many counselors there is safety. In Proverbs 12:15 and 15:22, it also shows that without counsel, the ways of the fool are right in his own eyes, showing that fools, which include prideful people or people that hate counseling from others, see that everything is right in their eyes even if what they believe is foolish.

We have the choice to listen, and if we listen Proverbs 9:9, 13:20, 19:20-21, and 20:18 tells us that we will grow in truth and we can become wise, that our purposes and our drives will be established. Through counsel we will go in the direction we need to go. The purpose of a child of God is to follow His will, meaning that our purpose to follow God's will, through His counsel, will be established, it will last, and it will stand in front of God.

In short, the Spirit of Counsel is what teaches, instructs, helps us, and shows us the way we need to follow in God's will. Just as the Spirit of Understanding is the key into God's wisdom, the Spirit of Counsel is also the key to the Spirit of Understanding, because by listening and following the Spirit of Counsel you will be directed towards the way of understanding your situation, and what is the proper choice, the good choice over the bad, what is good and not evil. As we have seen even until now, these Spirits are all interlocked with one another.

The Spirit of Might

- Judges 14:6 – And the Spirit of the LORD came mightily upon him, and he rent him as he would have rent a kid, and he had nothing in his hand: but he told not his father or his mother what he had done.
- Judges 14:19a – And the Spirit of the LORD came upon him, and he went down to Ashkelon, and slew thirty men of them…
- Judges 15:14 – And when he came unto Lehi, the Philistines shouted against him: and the Spirit of the LORD came mightily upon him, and the cords that were upon his arms became as flax that was burnt with fire, and his bands loosed from off his hands.
- 1 Chronicles 29:11-12 – Thine, O LORD is the greatness, and the power, and the glory, and the victory, and the majesty: for all that is in the heaven and in the earth is thine; thine is the kingdom, O LORD, and thou art exalted as head above all. Both riches and honour come of thee, and thou reignest over all; and in thine hand is power and might; and in thine hand it is to make great, and to give strength unto all.

- 2 Chronicles 20:6 – And said, O LORD God of our fathers, art not thou God in heaven? And rulest not thou over all the kingdoms of the heathen? And in thine hand is there not power and might, so that none is able to withstand thee?
- Micah 3:8 – On the other hand I am filled with power–With the Spirit of the LORD–And with justice and courage To make known to Jacob his rebellious act, Even to Israel his sin.
- Zechariah 4:6 – Then he answered and spake unto me, saying, This *is* the word of the LORD unto Zerubbabel, saying, Not by might, nor by power, but by my spirit, saith the LORD of hosts.
- Luke 24:49 – "And behold, I am sending forth the promise of My Father upon you; but you are to stay in the city until you are clothed with power from on high."
- Acts 1:8 – …but you will receive power when the Holy Spirit has come upon you; and you shall be My witnesses both in Jerusalem, and in all Judea and Samaria, and even to the remotest part of the earth.
- Acts 6:8 – And Stephen, full of grace and power, was performing great wonders and signs among the people.
- Acts 10:38 – "You know of Jesus of Nazareth, how God anointed Him with the Holy Spirit and with power, and how He went about doing good and healing all who were oppressed by the devil, for God was with Him.
- Romans 15:19 – in the power of signs and wonders, in the power of the Spirit; so that from Jerusalem and round about as far as Illyricum I have fully preached the gospel of Christ.
- 1 Corinthians 2:4 – and my message and my preaching were not in persuasive words of wisdom, but in demonstration of the Spirit and of power…

- 2 Corinthians 10:4 – (For the weapons of our warfare are not carnal, but mighty through God to the pulling down of strong holds Casting down imaginations, and every high thing that exalteth itself against the knowledge of God, and bringing into captivity every thought to the obedience of Christ; ...
- Ephesians 3:16 – That he would grant you, according to the riches of his glory, to be strengthened with might by his Spirit in the inner man; ...
- 2 Timothy 1:7 – For God has not given us a spirit of timidity, but of power and love and discipline.

Have you ever in your life, been in a situation of *trying* to do God's will but not succeeding? What I mean by this is, trying to do what He has called you to do or seeing something that should be brought up and spoken about, or needing to preach the Word of God how it is written – being sharper than a two edged sword speaking the truth and going through the bush, rather than around it. But no matter how hard your tried, you didn't have the courage, the nerve, the strength to do what you needed to do, or say, or go where He had called you. This is what the Spirt of Might (strength, power) is for and where it comes in to help us.

Before moving forward, I need to define Might and Power. Some Bible translations use power or strength interchangeably, but power/strength means that there is a limit to your power, only as a capacity to do what you need to do. While 'might' in the Bible is considered unmeasurable - the limit of God which, as we know, actually has no limit. The power that is given to us is a portion of the unlimited Might of God, through the Spirit. This power that is given is for us as His children to do His will.

In Judges 14:6, it says that Samson had the Spirit of the Lord come 'mightily' upon him and the power given to him was so powerful that he was able to tear the lion apart with ease. In Judges 15:14, it says that when the Spirit of the Lord came 'mightily' upon him, that he was able to break a cord/rope as if it was burnt flax. If we consider even a ¼ inch rope, it requires more than a 1100 pounds of strength to break it, as 1100 pounds is the safe load. During Bible times, rope was closer to three-quarter size which had about 10,000 pounds as a safe load. And if you've ever touched burnt flax, you know it just falls apart in your hands.

All this means that this might, the power given, was so powerful that the cord came off as if it wasn't even there.

In 1 Chronicles, it is written that this might is to give strength to all (His believers), in 2 Chronicles this might is so great that no one can stand against God, and when He pours it out on us it will also mean that none can stand against us. Just as Micah 3:8 says: he was filled with power from the Spirit of the Lord that gave him courage to go and tell Jacob his rebellious act and Israel his sins.

In Luke 24, the Apostles are told to not leave until they receive power through the Holy Spirit. Also, in Acts 1:8 it speaks about how this power will help them be Witnesses. This Spirit of Might will help you be courageous to be able to tell others about their sins and to repent, give you courage to let others know when they are rebellious against God and not following the Lord. Allow you to be a true witness for God, to tell others with power and courage and strength about your Lord and God, so you will not be ashamed, humiliated, embarrassed, or uncomfortable for the work of God.

In Acts 6:8, Stephen, filled with power, was able to do signs and wonders for the Lord God. And Romans 10 as well writes of the power that gives us the capability to preach the Gospel. The Spirit of Might is what is given to us, as sons and daughters of God, to do His will, to do the calling He has called us to do. To do it without fear, without anxiety, without struggling or concerns. Others may not like what you say or do, but the will of God many times takes us out of our comfort zone.

If we do the will of God, that is all that matters. The Spirit of Might gives us the courage and power to overcome all, with all our strength, body, soul, and Spirit according to God's will.

The Spirit of the Lord

- Isaiah 61:1 – The Spirit of the Lord GOD is upon me; because the LORD hath anointed me to preach good tidings unto the meek; he hath sent me to bind up the brokenhearted, to proclaim liberty to the captives, and the opening of the prison to them that are bound; …
- Isaiah 63:14 – As a beast goeth down into the valley, the Spirit of the LORD caused him to rest: so didst thou lead thy people, to make thyself a glorious name.
- Ezekiel 37:14 – And shall put my spirit in you, and ye shall live, and I shall place you in your own land: then shall ye know that I the LORD have spoken it, and performed it, saith the LORD.
- Joel 2:28 – And it shall come to pass afterward, that I will pour out my spirit upon all flesh; and your sons and your

daughters shall prophesy, your old men shall dream dreams, your young men shall see visions...

- Luke 4:18 – The Spirit of the Lord is upon me, because he hath anointed me to preach the gospel to the poor; he hath sent me to heal the brokenhearted, to preach deliverance to the captives, and recovering of sight to the blind, to set at liberty them that are bruised...

- John 16:8 – And when he is come, he will reprove the world of sin, and of righteousness, and of judgment...

- Romans 8:2 – For the law of the Spirit of life in Christ Jesus hath made me free from the law of sin and death.

- Romans 8:10 – And if Christ be in you, the body is dead because of sin; but the Spirit is life because of righteousness.

- Romans 15:16 – That I should be the minister of Jesus Christ to the Gentiles, ministering the gospel of God, that the offering up of the Gentiles might be acceptable, being sanctified by the Holy Ghost.

- 1 Corinthians 12 – *These verses speak about the nine Gifts of the Holy Spirit*

- 2 Corinthians 3:17- Now the Lord is that Spirit: and where the Spirit of the Lord is, there is liberty.

- Galatians 4:6 – And because ye are sons, God hath sent forth the Spirit of his Son into your hearts, crying, Abba, Father.

- Galatians 5:22-23 – But the fruit of the Spirit is love, joy, peace, longsuffering, gentleness, goodness, faith, Meekness, temperance: against such there is no law.

The Spirit of the Lord has many functions and duties that it accomplishes in us and through us. In this explanation of the Spirit of the Lord, we will cover some functions of the Lord's Spirit, but we will cover more when we will talk about purposes

32

or roles of the Spirit of the Lord. In Isaiah 61:1, it says that when the Spirit of the Lord came upon him, he was preaching, healing the broken-hearted, and proclaiming liberty over the captives. This specific Spirit helps us preach the Gospel and then to heal the broken-hearted/hopeless people which are in despair, in anguish, in pain; this is the Spirit which can heal.

The Spirit of the Lord also proclaims liberty/freedom over the captives. This means that if you feel chained down, a hostage, imprisoned, in bondage, or enslaved the Spirit of the Lord will set you free and proclaim liberty over you and you shall be freed/delivered in Jesus Christ. Just as in Isaiah 63:14 - it is the Spirit which brings rest to you, in your situations and problems. In Ezekiel 37:14 and Romans 8:10 it talks about the Spirit of the Lord bringing life to us and in us. Many times, we feel dead, in life and within us; without the Lord Christ in us, we have no meaning in life, no meaning of how our life should be, but the Spirit of the Lord brings Life, an eternal life.

Another function given through the Spirit of the Lord is in Joel 2:28, where it states that it brings prophecy, dreams, and visions. One of the most common verses known and used is John 16:8, which says, when He (Spirit of the Lord) comes, He will convict the world of sin, of righteousness, and of judgement. This signifies that He will convict us. Have you ever felt in your heart a conviction, a feeling of guilt and blame for something you have done? This is the Spirit of the Lord working in you. In our lives there are many times when we might do something, and as soon as we have done it, we feel as if something is wrong - we have a uneasiness; this is the Lord's Spirit that is convicting us of what we have done.

Romans 15:16 says the Holy Spirit will also sanctify us, which is consecration, being made Holy through Him. It is what cleanses us of our mistakes, sins, iniquity, and transgressions that we have committed in our lives. The Spirit of the Lord (Galatians 4) is also what allows us to call God, Father, as 'Abba, Father.' It is what brings us into a relationship with the Father. Also, in Galatians, it speaks about the fruits of the Spirit, which is another function we will cover later as well. The Spirit of the Lord is an amazing, wonderful Spirit with many functions for us, which help us have a peaceful life, a life with joy, a life with power, and much more.

I hope that reading about the seven Spirits of the Lord has helped you realize who is our Lord, the Creator of all, the King of Kings. With these verses from the Word of God, I hope it has given you more insight into wisdom, knowledge, and understanding of the seven Spirits of the Lord. I hope it has made you crave and desire to be able to ask and receive them in your life, through studying, prayer, and meditation of the Word of God.

Let the Spirit of Fear bring you into a state of awe and reverence for our God, the almighty King of Kings.

May the Spirit of Counsel help you receive the proper advice and guidance.

The Spirit of Wisdom, Knowledge, and Understanding will be available to you when you devote yourself to the Word of God.

With the Spirit of Might you will not fail when it comes to spreading the good Word and leading others to everlasting life.

And the Spirit of the Lord will keep you close to the 'Abba, Father,' ensuring that your efforts in His will do not go unfulfilled.

Reading and studying the seven Spirits of the Lord, I pray that it has encouraged you, and given you confidence, power in the Spirit of Might to move forward and ask to receive them in you, to do the will of the Father in the name of Jesus Christ through the Holy Ghost. To experience and comprehend the magnificent Wisdom, Knowledge, Understanding, Counsel, Might, and Fear of God and the Spirit of the Lord to the fullest extent in your life and around you.

If we want to be able to do the will of God in our life in the path that has been drawn out, we must start growing spiritually in Christ. Grow in our relationship and fellowship in Christ. To start sanctifying our life through the Spirit of the Lord. Once we start applying what we know, we can start growing and experiencing all sorts of wonderful miracles and healings and many other things in our life in the will of God.

Notes

Part 2:
Seven Eyes of the
Seven Spirits

This specific subject is something that many do not understand. The reason behind this is because it *seems* as if the Word of God doesn't have much about what these seven eyes do. I would like to take you step-by-step, with the Word of God, to explain the seven eyes of the spirits. I would like to go into more detail about what these specific seven eyes do.

We first need to determine what 'eyes' do in general. You and I use our eyes, this organ of the visual system, to look upon objects, people, or nature; we use our eyes to observe, perceive, and to distinguish all.

As we now know, the seven spirits are the seven-fold of the Holy Spirit, and the Holy Ghost is the Spirit of God. The seven eyes of the seven spirits are the eyes of our God and these eyes have insight, observe, see all, perceive all, and distinguish all.

You may ask then, what do they observe, see, perceive, or distinguish? The eyes look upon everything we do internally and externally. These seven eyes observe what we look at (Eyes), what we speak (Mouth), what we hear (Ears), what we think (Brain), what we desire (Heart/Soul), where we go (Feet), and what we do (Hands).

When we look in the Word of God, we will see that these seven specific things are consistently being monitored and warned about - what we think or see or hear, etc. In Luke 8:17, it says that everything that is secret or hidden will come to be known and manifested. Another passage, in Romans 2:16, says that the day will come when our God will judge the secrets of men by Jesus Christ. These are two passages that show that everything we try to hide or do in secret, to keep from family (sister, brother, parents), friends, or spouses/significant others will come to be known during the day of Judgment, when God will reveal what was done.

When we truly think about this, we realize that we can hide and keep things in secret of what we hear, see, speak, think, desire, do, or where we go. The only way these can be brought to light and be known in judgment is if God knows what is being done at all times in your life. This is possible because the divine insight of God will be constantly and persistently looking at everything we say, hear, think, desire, do, and where we go.

Let's go and see a few passages in the Bible that speak about each eye's observation. What we will realize is that throughout scripture, these are the seven things that God tells us not to do or to watch out for, to make sure we protect ourselves.

The reason is because these parts of us are what can take us to places and situations in life that lead us away from God.

The Eye of Eyes

- Proverbs 4:20-21,25 - My son, attend to my words; incline thine ear unto my sayings. Let them not depart from thine eyes; keep them in the midst of thine heart. (25) Let thine eyes look right on, and let thine eyelids look straight before thee.

- Matthew 6:22-23 - The light of the body is the eye: if therefore thine eye be single, thy whole body shall be full of light. But if thine eye be evil, thy whole body shall be full of darkness. If therefore the light that is in thee be darkness, how great is that darkness!

- Matthew 5:28,29 - But I say unto you, that whosoever looketh on a woman to lust after her hath committed adultery with her already in his heart. And if thy right eye offend thee, pluck it out, and cast it from thee: for it is profitable for thee that one of thy members should perish, and not that thy whole body should be cast into hell.

- Acts 28:27 - For the heart of this people is waxed gross, and their ears are dull of hearing, and their eyes have they closed; lest they should see with their eyes, and hear with their ears, and understand with their heart, and should be converted, and I should heal them.

As we see here, the passage of Proverbs 4 says that our eyes should not depart from His words, and we should keep them consistently in our eyesight, that we should look forward at all times. During our lives, we should be consistently looking at God's words and His will. When we do this, it allows our eyes to not wander where they should not and to be fixated on what they should be, which is God.

We see in the passage of Matthew 6 that it tells us that the light of our body is our eyes. If we look at darkness and perceive with our eyes what we should not, we will become filled with evil and darkness, but if we keep our eyes clean/clear and spiritually discerning then our whole body will be full of light (which is pure and clean, holy in front of God).

We know, for example, that when we continue looking at what we should not, this is what happens; our mind is consistently thinking of things it should not. This happens because we give the devil opportunity to fill our thoughts with evil things and this started by us looking with our eyes. The same is true if we consistently read the Word of God and look upon Him - we then always meditate on Him in our thoughts.

When we continue and look at Matthew 5, we see that the act, or sin, of adultery starts first from seeing/observing with the eyes and then, when there is lust in your heart, you commit the act. In this passage, it tells us that it is better to pluck out the eyes, for it is better to lose a member than the whole body. This refers to the body of Christ, but at the same time we can use this passage for us as well.

For example, if you know for a fact that because you use your smartphone too much it takes you away from fulfilling God's will - because you fill you head with games, social media, and other apps - it is better for you to remove that distraction by removing your smartphone and perhaps getting a flip phone. If you realize that your TV is taking you in the wrong direction, it is better to remove it and live without it, because it is better not to perish from a worldly, material thing but instead have everlasting life.

When we look at the last passage, Acts 28, it tells us that "their hearts have become waxed and their eyes have been closed to the truth." If we allow ourselves to become numb to the truth, we also will not to listen to the Word of God and will not obey the conviction in our hearts when the Holy Spirit speaks. The more we do not want to listen or obey what we know is right, the more we will eventually become numb to it and it will have no effect on us.

This will then cause us to look upon what we should not be perceiving with our eyes. What made us feel guilty and convicted before, will no longer make us feel that way and it will make us think that it has become good now. This is what causes the children of God to become numb and live a lukewarm life, even if not totally cold. Of course, this may lead you to forsaking the living God completely. We must stay attentive and make sure that what we observe with our eyes is holy and clean in front of our God.

The Second Eye (Ears)

- Provers 4:20 - My son, attend to my words; incline thine ear unto my sayings.
- Acts 28:26-27 - Saying, Go unto this people, and say, Hearing ye shall hear, and shall not understand; and seeing ye shall see, and not perceive: For the heart of this people is waxed gross, and their ears are dull of hearing, and their eyes have they closed; lest they should see with their eyes, and hear with their ears, and understand with their heart, and should be converted, and I should heal them.

- James 3:3-6 -Behold, we put bits in the horses' mouths, that they may obey us; and we turn about their whole body. Behold also the ships, which though they be so great, and are driven of fierce winds, yet are they turned about with a very small helm, whithersoever the governor listeth. Even so the tongue is a little member, and boasteth great things. Behold, how great a matter a little fire kindleth! And the tongue is a fire, a world of iniquity: so is the tongue among our members, that it defileth the whole body, and setteth on fire the course of nature; and it is set on fire of hell.
- Matthew 13:9 - Who hath ears to hear, let him hear.
- Luke 8:11-15 - Now the parable is this: The seed is the word of God. Those by the way side are they that hear; then cometh the devil, and taketh away the word out of their hearts, lest they should believe and be saved. They on the rock are they, which, when they hear, receive the word with joy; and these have no root, which for a while believe, and in time of temptation fall away. And that which fell among thorns are they, which, when they have heard, go forth, and are choked with cares and riches and pleasures of this life, and bring no fruit to perfection. But that on the good ground are they, which in an honest and good heart, having heard the word, keep it, and bring forth fruit with patience.
- Hebrew 3:12 - Take heed, brethren, lest there be in any of you an evil heart of unbelief, in departing from the living God.

Our ears have a great impact on how we act in our lives; we don't usually think of our ears as having much power, but they do. Much in our lives happens because of what we hear and decide to believe. In Matthew 13, it tells us, 'who has an ear to hear, let him or her hear.' We realize that Jesus many times said, 'who has an ear, to listen.' This is because the ear has great impact on us. Proverbs 4 advises the reader to attend to the words of God and incline their ears to His sayings. We, as Christians, must incline our ears to what God has said. There are too many times that we incline our ears not to God but to men which lead us astray.

We read in the passage of Acts 28 that 'their ears have become dull' - this term is perfect here. Something becomes dull the more you use it. We need to look at it this way - the more you hear someone keep on telling you something that you do not agree with, the more you become tired of it, or dull to it. Becoming dull to the teaching of God is dangerous. You might say, why or how would someone do this?

When you like what you're doing - you like feeling lust, desire, being in addictions, speaking gossip, or creating drama - and someone continues to tell you it is bad, you will eventually just not listen and become dull to that advice or tell yourself that everyone does this, it is normal and not wrong. You try to rationalize what is normal to man and not to God.

In addition to this, the passage in James 3 is not only about speaking but also about listening. This passage speaks about what the tongue can do, but for it to be able to do something, someone must also be listening. Otherwise, he will speak, and no one will hear. For example, we know that we should not gossip, but even when someone speaks about someone else you should not listen for then you are partaking in the gossip by just listening. This is because after we listen, it will cause us to make judgments towards someone or make us think of them wrongfully or it may make us desire something or do something we should not.

If you are not strong in the teaching of God, you may listen to someone else's doctrine or teaching, and this can lead you astray. Just because someone made a strong point for something can make you believe in it even if it is wrong - this happens because you heard with your ears.

Luke 8 speaks about someone that hears the Word of God and the devil comes and takes it out of their heart. What we need to realize here is that it is talking about someone that did hear it and it already went into their heart (desire, soul). This means it is someone that took it to heart already and then the devil comes and takes it away from them so they will not believe. How is this possible?

The Word of God tells us that they will come with enticing words and seducing words of teaching and doctrines that lead away from God's true word. This is possible because we allow ourselves to listen with our ears and if it sounds more attractive, or seems like an easier way of teaching for following God, you might just do it because it makes it easier on you. We must not have an evil heart to depart from God. We must stay strong in truth which means that we must listen to the Word of God.

The Third Eye (Mouth)
- Psalms 141:3 - Set a watch, O LORD, before my mouth; keep the door of my lips.
- Proverbs 4:24 - Put away from thee a froward mouth, and perverse lips put far from thee.

47

- Proverbs 18:21 - Death and life are in the power of the tongue: and they that love it shall eat the fruit thereof.
- Ecclesiastes 5:2 - Be not rash with thy mouth, and let not thine heart be hasty to utter any thing before God: for God is in heaven, and thou upon earth: therefore let thy words be few.
- James 3:3-6 - Behold, we put bits in the horses' mouths, that they may obey us; and we turn about their whole body. Behold also the ships, which though they be so great, and are driven of fierce winds, yet are they turned about with a very small helm, whithersoever the governor listeth. Even so the tongue is a little member, and boasteth great things. Behold, how great a matter a little fire kindleth! And the tongue is a fire, a world of iniquity: so is the tongue among our members, that it defileth the whole body, and setteth on fire the course of nature; and it is set on fire of hell.
- James 1:26 - If any man among you seem to be religious, and bridleth not his tongue, but deceiveth his own heart, this man's religion is vain.

In the Word of God, the mouth is given much power, which is understandable. Proverbs 18 tells us that our tongue has the power of death and life in it and they that love it shall eat the fruit of it. There are many passages in the Bible that show us that because of what someone said, death was brought to them; the most known of these cases would be that of Ananias and Sapphira. They, with their mouths, lied to the Holy Spirit and death was their punishment.

The same is true for life - the way we speak to others has the power to bring life. This is why it tells us in Proverbs 4 to put the forward mouth and perverse lips away from us because what we say will also judge us.

We need not to be rash or impulsive in how we speak but we need to be children of God, of few words, just as Ecclesiastes 5 says. Someone that is a child of God will wait to examine the situation they are in to see what is happening around them. They will wait upon the Holy Spirit to give them words and when they will speak it will be a few words, but they will be powerful and transformative to others around them. There are too many that speak hastily and with many words which leads to confusion and pridefulness. Their words are not powerful or transformative; they think they have all the answers yet have no impact at all.

We see in Scripture that Peter, with his mouth, denied Jesus Christ three times, just as it was predicted he would. The same goes for Judah: he accepted with his mouth to betray the Lord Jesus Christ for money. We also see how the scribes, with their words, blasphemed against the Holy Spirit. With our mouths we are able to worship, praise God, give thanks and glory to our living God, but with our mouths we are also able to betray, blasphemy, lie, slander, take God's name in vain, and to bring death.

David, in Psalms 141, tells the Lord to put a guard over his mouth and watch (observe) his lips to make sure what he said was just, pure, and right in front of God. Just as David did, we must put a guard and a watch for our mouths to make sure we do not speak against God. When we are able to learn from the Holy Spirit, when we are able to accept what He wants to speak to us, we will be able to start watching our mouths and become

49

someone that speaks life and power around us. The words we speak will be brought to light and what we speak will either bring life or death.

The Fourth Eye (Mind and Thoughts)

- Luke 5:22 - But when Jesus perceived their thoughts, he answering said unto them, What reason ye in your hearts?
- Romans 1:28 - And even as they did not like to retain God in their knowledge, God gave them over to a reprobate mind, to do those things which are not convenient; ...
- Romans 12:2 - And be not conformed to this world: but be ye transformed by the renewing of your mind, that ye may prove what is that good, and acceptable, and perfect, will of God.
- 1 Thessalonians 4:4 - That every one of you should know how to possess his vessel in sanctification and honour; ...

We see from many passages in the Word of God that Jesus says He knew what they were thinking or what their thoughts were. Luke 5 is one of the many passages where we see this, that Jesus perceived their thoughts, and because of this He also knew what was in their hearts. The heart and mind work together many times, because for something to already be a desire in your soul, which is your heart, you must also have thought about it in your mind to see if it was worth enough to have it in your heart.

Romans 1 says that they did not want to retain or keep God in their knowledge. Knowledge is kept in your mind. This passage refers to the consequences of unbelief. We may say this only refers to non-believers, but we see in Hebrew 3:12 that it speaks to brothers in Christ - to not have an evil heart of unbelief

50

in God and to depart from Him. This shows us that if we eventually leave the faith because of our unbelief from an evil heart, we may end up in the consequences of this passage: the Lord will give us over to what we want and what is not right.

Romans 12 says that we should not be conformed to what this world is or what it has to offer us but instead to have our mind renewed and transformed. We must not allow what this world is offering in their lies and deceit, telling us that it is good or pleasurable, we must not ponder on what will eventually burn and leave after a breath but we must stay firm and let our thoughts meditate on God, to ponder and think consistently of what our Lord wants from us. In 1 Thessalonians 4 it tells us to possess our vessel. The word of 'possess' here means 'under control' - we do not control our minds with our hearts, but we tell our hearts what to desire, we give it a job from our mind. We must be strong and sanctify our minds and, once we do this, we will be able to be in control of our mind.

The Fifth Eye (Heart)

- Psalms 51:10 - Create in me a clean heart, O God; and renew a right spirit within me.
- Psalms 66:18 - If I regard iniquity in my heart, the Lord will not hear me.
- Proverbs 4:21,23 - Let them not depart from thine eyes; keep them in the midst of thine heart. 23. Keep thy heart with all diligence; for out of it are the issues of life.
- Matthew 5:28 - But I say unto you, That whosoever looketh on a woman to lust after her hath committed adultery with her already in his heart.

- Hebrew 3:12 - Take heed, brethren, lest there be in any of you an evil heart of unbelief, in departing from the living God.

We see that many times in our lives the heart is what controls many things and not the mind. The heart is part of the soul or the soul is the heart, as we have seen. The heart is what desires, wants, and craves. This is something that we all have experienced – for example, we know that we shouldn't eat something, but we do it because we crave it. Or when we go to a store and would like to buy a specific shirt, pair of pants, hair tie, or suit, and we know (in our mind) that we do not have the money for it, but we desire it so much that we still buy it.

Another example would be when you are with a group of people and you would like to say something but you know (mind) you should not but you desire to tell them, so you do (which then becomes gossip). These are just a few simple examples among many. When we listen to our heart's desire, many times, it leads us towards pain and suffering and there are consequences for what we have done.

In the passage of Psalms 51, it says 'create in me a clean heart,' a heart that follows Christ no matter what and not what I want. In Psalms 66, it says that if you keep (hide) iniquity in your heart, the Lord will not hear you. When we allow our heart to be dirty or hide sins rather than repent from what we have done, our Lord will not hear us. We need to start repenting and keeping our hearts clean.

In the passage of Proverbs 4, it tells us to not allow the words of God to leave our hearts; we must always keep the Lord's words in our hearts, it must be what we desire and crave for it is the Word of God in our life. If we keep our hearts with diligence in this way, life will burst forth from our hearts for all to see.

Conversely, just as we see in Matthew 5, we can also commit sins in our hearts, such as adultery, for from our heart many things flow out. As Jesus said, it is not what comes in that defiles a man but what comes out, and what comes out is many times what is in our heart. That is why, what is in our heart will define us.

What we desire and what is in our hearts will also show on the outside, the way we speak, the way we act, the way we dress and everything else. An evil heart can also make you depart from God (and you cannot depart from someone unless you are with them in the first place). We must keep guard on our hearts, keep it clean, and ask God to renew it and make it want what He desires for you.

The Sixth Eye (Feet)

- Proverbs 4:26-27 - Ponder the path of thy feet, and let all thy ways be established. Turn not to the right hand nor to the left: remove thy foot from evil.
- Ecclesiastes 5:1 - Keep thy foot when thou goest to the house of God, and be more ready to hear, than to give the sacrifice of fools: for they consider not that they do evil.
- Romans 12:2 - And be not conformed to this world: but be ye transformed by the renewing of your mind, that ye may prove what is that good, and acceptable, and perfect, will of God.

- Hebrew 3:12 - Take heed, brethren, lest there be in any of you an evil heart of unbelief, in departing from the living God.

Throughout our life, our feet take us in many places: work, school, stores, family and friends' homes, and church but it can also take us to clubs, bars, and adult areas among others where we shouldn't be. Our feet can lead us in areas we need to be and other areas that we shouldn't be in. When we look in the passage of Proverbs 4, it tells us to ponder the path of our feet. To 'ponder' is to think and meditate where you are going with your feet. And it continues in the passage, saying to establish your ways; to establish means to be created and followed in God's way.

We need to make firm our paths where our feet are going, then we must make sure that our feet are leading us to everlasting life and not to everlasting damnation. It is very important where we go. That is why it tells us not to turn to the right or left; this is saying, do not try to make excuses for where your feet were by saying it was the right or left side doing it. But remove, or take yourself away, from the path of evil and onto the path of God, for where you go matters and it will be shown in the consequences.

In Ecclesiastes 5, it says for us to guard our feet when we enter into the house of God. This passage relates to priesthood, but we, as children of God, have been put into the priesthood. It says we must be on guard, protect ourselves, and always make sure we are on the path of God. It tells us not to give sacrifice and not go and do what fools do, for they do evil without knowing it. We must be on guard, for if we are not, we may end up departing from God with our feet in the direction of sin, transgression, and evilness.

When we are renewed and transformed in our minds, this will also allow us to start knowing what God's will is for us and give us access to start following God. We will start stepping in the footprints of Jesus Christ to act as He did, to speak as He did, and to love as He did. This will allow us to walk in His ways. When we start walking in His ways it will be known to others as well. If we do not follow in His steps it will also be known, for we will not represent Christ. Where you and I walk matters because where you went will be judged when brought in front of God.

The Seventh Eye (Hands)

- Isaiah 59:1-3 - Behold, the LORD's hand is not shortened, that it cannot save; neither his ear heavy, that it cannot hear: But your iniquities have separated between you and your God, and your sins have hid his face from you, that he will not hear. For your hands are defiled with blood, and your fingers with iniquity; your lips have spoken lies, your tongue hath muttered perverseness.
- 1 Timothy 2:8 - I will therefore that men pray every where, lifting up holy hands, without wrath and doubting.
- Proverbs 4:26-27 - Ponder the path of thy feet, and let all thy ways be established. Turn not to the right hand nor to the left: remove thy foot from evil.
- Matthew 5:30 - And if thy right hand offend thee, cut it off, and cast it from thee: for it is profitable for thee that one of thy members should perish, and not that thy whole body should be cast into hell.

- Romans 12:2 - And be not conformed to this world: but be ye transformed by the renewing of your mind, that ye may prove what is that good, and acceptable, and perfect, will of God.
- 1 Timothy 5:22 - Lay hands suddenly on no man, neither be partaker of other men's sins: keep thyself pure.

We come to the last of the seven eyes which represents the hands. The feet take us and our hands do for us. Our hands can either be in sin or they can be holy. In the passage of Isaiah 59, it tells us that the Lord's hand is not shortened so that it cannot save. The problem comes to us, it says, that our iniquities have separated us from God and that our sins have hid His face from us because our hands are defiled with blood. When we act and make others sin then we have their blood on our hands. For we know, as Scripture says in Ezekiel 33:6, that if the watchman sees something coming and does not warn the others and someone is taken away, the blood of that one will be on the watchman's hands.

We are watchmen of God; when we see others sin and we do not warn them that they are sinning and allow them in their ways, it will also fall on us.

Hebrews 10:26 says that if we continue in sin after the knowledge of truth, there is no more sacrifice for sin. The first sacrifice for sin was payed for by the blood of Jesus Christ. When we continue in sin, since there is no more sacrifice for it, we ourselves now will need to pay for our sins. This is not to say that there is no *forgiveness in repentance* but that now you have to pay the punishment of sin. This is why the Word of God tells us that we will be judged now so that we will not be judged at the end with the world.

In the passage of Matthew 5, it tells us that if our hand makes us sin it is better for us to cut it off and cast it from ourselves. The passage in 1 Timothy 5 tells us not to lay hands suddenly (swiftly or quickly) on anyone, neither be partakers of other people's sin. It tells us to beware and don't go around laying hands and be part of what others do in their sins, but instead be pure and keep yourself from them, watch, and be discerning of what is happening. We must be transformed and, once we are transformed, what we do with our hands will become the will of the Father. Once we are in the will of the Father, we will be able to lift up holy hands without wrath or doubting, for we will be in His will.

Conclusion

When we read in Scripture, throughout the whole Bible, we will see that God always refers to one of these seven areas. One of these seven areas is consistently being observed and watched to see what we are doing. The Lord our God either refers to our heart, eyes, ears, mouth, thoughts, hands, or feet. We need to start looking at ourselves and really examine every part of our lives. You need to start looking and seeing if you are hearing what you need to through your ears and start removing out of your life what is evil, so you will only hear what is right and pure in front of God. If this means new friends or departing from family, you must let them go; if they do not change, you must leave. We must be willing to sacrifice what we need to so that we can do the will of God and not fall into gossip, slander, or other sinful actions in front of God.

We must examine our mouths and start removing what we must to have a clean mouth; if you are the one gossiping, it is time to remove gossip out of your mouth. If you were the one lying, it is time to remove that as well.

It is time to put yourself to a test and see if you fail in what is pure in front of God. If you stand to His standards and not the world's standards. It is time to start looking into what is in our hearts and thoughts. If we desire what is not of God, we need to start crucifying our flesh and start saying we will follow You, our God. It is time to start removing evil thoughts and start meditating on the Word of God which will bring good, pure, and righteous thoughts, holy in front of God.

We need to put our hands and feet into examination and start seeing if our feet are bringing us in areas that we should not be going, in areas that sin is waiting for us, where temptation is. You need to start looking and seeing where your hands are, what they are doing, and if are they doing what is not good in front of God. If you start realizing that your feet and hands are going against what God has been saying and telling you to do, then it is time for you to start cutting off what is corrupt in your life to start fulfilling God's holy plan for yourself. Even if you must start sacrificing what you thought you never would need to.

In the end time, when we will come before God, all that was hidden in your mind and that was hidden in your heart will come to light. Anything that you have heard, spoken, and seen with your eyes, that you thought was hidden that no one would ever see, will come to be visible. Wherever you have gone and whatever you have done hidden from everyone, and thought you were fooling everyone, shall come into the light and be known -

all the shame, embarrassment, guilt, and resentment you were hoping will not come to pass, will come to pass.

For the divine insight of God with His Seven Eyes, of the Seven Spirits of God, will be looking, observing, and discerning everything that you have done. Everything that you thought would never come to light, everything that you have kept in secret. You might have lost finances, family, friends and material things to keep these hidden so that no one will know. A time will come that it will be taken from the deepest and darkest areas and it will be put on a hill to be in the light. It is time for us to realize that God observes all, He sees all, and He perceives all with His divine insight of the Seven Spirits of the Lord.

Notes

Part 3:
Symbols of the
Holy Spirit

Dove – Symbolizes Meekness, Gentleness, Peace of God

- Matthew 3:16 - And Jesus, when he was baptized, went up straightway out of the water: and, lo, the heavens were opened unto him, and he saw the Spirit of God descending like a dove, and lighting upon him...
- John 1:32-33 - And John bare record, saying, I saw the Spirit descending from heaven like a dove, and it abode upon him. And I knew him not: but he that sent me to baptize with water, the same said unto me, Upon whom thou shalt see the Spirit descending, and remaining on him, the same is he which baptizeth with the Holy Ghost.

The Dove is one of the symbols or representations of the Holy Spirit; just as a dove is gentle, the Holy Spirit is as well. Just as Matthew wrote about the Holy Spirit descending onto Jesus, He wants to come and descend onto us. The dove is a symbol of peace, indicating that, when the Holy Spirit comes upon you and I, we will have spiritual peace in our lives. This bird was considered a clean animal and a symbol of purity under the Law of the Old Testament. When the dove, the Holy Spirit, comes, He will bring peace and purity to a child of God - into your life, friendships, and in your spiritual life.

Seal – Symbolizes the Mark of God on His children

- Ephesians 1:13 - In whom ye also trusted, after that ye heard the word of truth, the gospel of your salvation: in whom also after that ye believed, ye were sealed with that holy Spirit of promise...
- Ephesians 4:30 - And grieve not the holy Spirit of God, whereby ye are sealed unto the day of redemption.
- 2 Corinthians 1:22 - Who hath also sealed us, and given the earnest of the Spirit in our hearts.

A seal is also used as a symbol of the Holy Spirit, indicating the moment when an individual receives Jesus Christ as their personal savior and asks Him to come into their life. The Holy Spirit will be sealed upon him or her. This is a mark of God on the person indicating he or she is God's property that God has ownership over. A seal, just like in real life, is made not to be broken only in certain conditions. The seal of God is put on you for accepting Him as your Lord and God, but if you deny Him this seal can be broken; if you live an unrighteous life and depart from the living God, this seal can be broken.

Oil – Symbolizes the anointment of God

- Luke 4:18 - The Spirit of the Lord is upon me, because he hath anointed me to preach the gospel to the poor; he hath sent me to heal the brokenhearted, to preach deliverance to the captives, and recovering of sight to the blind, to set at liberty them that are bruised...

- Acts 10:38 - How God anointed Jesus of Nazareth with the Holy Ghost and with power: who went about doing good, and healing all that were oppressed of the devil; for God was with him.

- 1 Samuel 16:3 - And call Jesse to the sacrifice, and I will shew thee what thou shalt do: and thou shalt anoint unto me him whom I name unto thee.

- Isaiah 61:1 - The Spirit of the Lord GOD is upon me; because the LORD hath anointed me to preach good tidings unto the meek; he hath sent me to bind up the brokenhearted, to proclaim liberty to the captives, and the opening of the prison to them that are bound; ...

- James 5:14 - Is any sick among you? let him call for the elders of the church; and let them pray over him, anointing him with oil in the name of the Lord...

- 2 Corinthians 1:21- Now he which stablisheth us with you in Christ, and hath anointed us, is God; ...

- 1 John 2:27 - But the anointing which ye have received of him abideth in you, and ye need not that any man teach you: but as the same anointing teacheth you of all things, and is truth, and is no lie, and even as it hath taught you, ye shall abide in him.

- Hebrew 1:9 - Thou hast loved righteousness, and hated iniquity; therefore God, even thy God, hath anointed thee with the oil of gladness above thy fellows.

As we see in the passages above, the anointment is an indication that the Holy Spirit has been put on you or that you

66

have received it. The anointment of the Holy Spirit will allow you to do the will of God in your life; for example, it can help you in preaching the Word. You can also learn from the anointment, indicating that the Holy Spirit in your life will teach you and show you the truth in such things as pastoring, evangelizing, and much more. It will allow you to understand situations and to feel with others.

Wind – Symbolizes the renewal, revival, or resurrection power of God

- John 3:8 - The wind bloweth where it listeth, and thou hearest the sound thereof, but canst not tell whence it cometh, and whither it goeth: so is every one that is born of the Spirit.
- Acts 2:2 - And suddenly there came a sound from heaven as of a rushing mighty wind, and it filled all the house where they were sitting.

Wind brings renewal in the physical life, wind causes the weather to change, wind causes pollination, and brings about many other changes. John 3 shows us that this is what the Holy Spirit can do in our life; He will blow us in the direction we must go, to do the will of God. It will direct us in the way we must go, it will pull or nudge us just as the wind does, it brings life to us. If we don't have wind in our world, eventually, we will start dying, plants will start dying, as well as animals. Wind is what brings life.

Breath – Symbolizes the life of God given

- John 20:22 - And when he had said this, he breathed on them, and saith unto them, Receive ye the Holy Ghost...

- Genesis 2:7- And the LORD God formed man of the dust of the ground, and breathed into his nostrils the breath of life; and man became a living soul.
- Job 27:3 - All the while my breath is in me, and the spirit of God is in my nostrils; ...
- Job 33:4 - The spirit of God hath made me, and the breath of the Almighty hath given me life.

As we saw above, wind brings life, but breath is what keeps us living. Breath is the indication of life - as we see in Genesis 2, the passage tells us that the Lord breathed into his nostrils the breath of life. John 20 shows that Jesus breathed on them and told them to receive the Holy Spirit. This breath is life. We know and understand that if we do not breathe, we would die physically. Here it is the same concept: the Holy Spirit is our breath, without Him giving us breath we would pass away, for breath is life.

Rain – Symbolizes the Pouring of God's Blessing

- Hosea 10:12 - Sow to yourselves in righteousness, reap in mercy; break up your fallow ground: for it is time to seek the LORD, till he come and rain righteousness upon you.
- Joel 2:23 - Be glad then, ye children of Zion, and rejoice in the LORD your God: for he hath given you the former rain moderately, and he will cause to come down for you the rain, the former rain, and the latter rain in the first month.
- James 5:7 - Be patient therefore, brethren, unto the coming of the Lord. Behold, the husbandman waiteth for the precious fruit of the earth, and hath long patience for it, until he receive the early and latter rain.

There are times we feel the pouring of God's blessing upon us. Just as rain comes and goes. When it rains, it brings blessings on the land and it can bring life and new growth there. There are many passages in Scripture that speak about God pouring His blessing out; the word 'pouring' can also be translated as 'rain or raining'. In Hosea, it says He will rain righteousness upon them. This is showing a blessing of what is right.

In Joel, it writes that He gave rain moderately, now He will allow rain to come yet again, a rain of blessing upon them. In James, it shows that they waited patiently for rain to come; this rain is a blessing of God on His people. If we want a blessing to come, we need to ask God to allow rain to come upon us.

Rivers – Symbolize the creating/generation/connection of God Power

- John 7:37-39 - In the last day, that great day of the feast, Jesus stood and cried, saying, If any man thirst, let him come unto me, and drink. He that believeth on me, as the scripture hath said, out of his belly shall flow rivers of living water. (But this spake he of the Spirit, which they that believe on him should receive: for the Holy Ghost was not yet given; because that Jesus was not yet glorified.).
- Psalms 1:3 - And he shall be like a tree planted by the rivers of water, that bringeth forth his fruit in his season; his leaf also shall not wither; and whatsoever he doeth shall prosper.

When we think about rivers, we think about a way of connecting one area to another and this brings life by generating or creating new life in other areas. This is the same way the symbol of the river is as the Holy Spirit. Those that have the Holy Spirit will have a river of living water, that river is a connection between you and the Father which brings life to you and generates you into being a new creation. Since the river of life comes out of you, it will also bring life by connecting you to others, to bring life to them as well. A living river will bring forth fruits in his season and what he will do will prosper, for the rivers will be flowing out from him. Rivers are a source of connection to bring life.

Water- Symbolizes the Life-Giving Power of God

- Ezekiel 36:25 - Then will I sprinkle clean water upon you, and ye shall be clean: from all your filthiness, and from all your idols, will I cleanse you.
- John 4:14 - But whosoever drinketh of the water that I shall give him shall never thirst; but the water that I shall give him shall be in him a well of water springing up into everlasting life.
- John 7:38 - He that believeth on me, as the scripture hath said, out of his belly shall flow rivers of living water.
- Isaiah 12:3, 44:3 - Therefore with joy shall ye draw water out of the wells of salvation. 44:3 - For I will pour water upon him that is thirsty, and floods upon the dry ground: I will pour my spirit upon thy seed, and my blessing upon thine offspring…

Earlier we were speaking about life as breath from the Holy Spirit and of rivers and rain. We know that rivers start from a source of water and rain comes from water that evaporates and condenses into clouds. Now, water is the source of the river and of the rain meaning it is the source of life. The water is the source of salvation into everlasting life. This water does not just bring salvation and everlasting life, but it will also cleanse us.

The Holy Spirit is the source and if we hold the Holy Spirit, we shall never thirst for we shall have this water source in us.

Wine – Symbolizes the Joy of Newness

- Matthew 9:16-17 - No man putteth a piece of new cloth unto an old garment, for that which is put in to fill it up taketh from the garment, and the rent is made worse. Neither do men put new wine into old bottles: else the bottles break, and the wine runneth out, and the bottles perish: but they put new wine into new bottles, and both are preserved.

In this passage, it is written about how you can't put new cloth on an old one for, if you do, the old will break apart from the new. That is why it tells us that you can't put new wine in an old wine skin because the old wine skin is already stretched from fermentation; if you put new wine in it, it will over-stretch and burst the old wine skin. That is why when the Holy Spirit is put into you, you must be made anew already. This is saying that the old must be renewed to accept the new wine (Holy Spirit) - if not, it will cause problems between the old you (wineskin) and the Holy Spirit (new wine). Because of this you must be willing to accept the transformation to be renewed so that a new wine can be put into you. That is why we repent and accept Christ as our Lord, to become new.

Clothing – Symbolizes the empowerment of the Holy Spirit

- Luke 24:49 - And, behold, I send the promise of my Father upon you: but tarry ye in the city of Jerusalem, until ye be endued (clothed) with power from on high.

The Holy Spirit is referred to here as clothing. In our life, what we wear is also what we are. What I mean is that what is in your heart will be reflected also on the outside with how you act, speak, and dress. Clothing can make us feel new and people use clothing to make themselves a new person; in our generation, clothing shows the levels of society. When we have been clothed with the Holy Spirit, we will be a new person in authority and power, in a different position that we have been previously put in, for we have accepted our Lord.

Cloud – Symbolizes the Glory of God

- 2 Chronicles 5:13b - that then the house was filled with a cloud, even the house of the LORD; …
- Ezekiel 10:3-5 - Now the cherubims stood on the right side of the house, when the man went in; and the cloud filled the inner court. Then the glory of the LORD went up from the cherub, and stood over the threshold of the house; and the house was filled with the cloud, and the court was full of the brightness of the LORD's glory.
- 1 King 8:11 - So that the priests could not stand to minister because of the cloud: for the glory of the LORD had filled the house of the LORD.
- Luke 1:35 - And the angel answered and said unto her, The Holy Ghost shall come upon thee, and the power of the Highest shall overshadow thee: therefore also that holy thing which shall be born of thee shall be called the Son of God.

In all the passages above, we see that a cloud signifies the glory of God being present. When we have a dream, a vision or any other experience that the Lord allows us to have, clouds signify the glory of God being present in that area. We see in the passages above that a home was filled with a cloud and this was the glory of God. In 1 Kings, it shows that this cloud was so great that the priests could not stand to minister because the glory of God manifested so strongly in the temple.

Finger – Symbolizes the Holy Spirit Power in Judgement or Deliverance

- Luke 11:20 - But if I with the finger of God cast out devils, no doubt the kingdom of God is come upon you.
- Exodus 8:19 - Then the magicians said unto Pharaoh, This is the finger of God: and Pharaoh's heart was hardened, and he hearkened not unto them; as the LORD had said.
- John 8:6 - This they said, tempting him, that they might have to accuse him. But Jesus stooped down, and with his finger wrote on the ground, as though he heard them not.

The finger represents the power of God being on someone; this finger has power of judgment and/or deliverance. This passage shows the finger of God can cast out devils, indicating the power of deliverance. We have here, in these few passages, the power of God being shown through His finger and judgment in the passage of John 8, when Jesus wrote with His finger on the ground and they walked away - this too was a sign of judgment for the rest there, for what was going on.

Hand – Symbolizes the power and the work/action of God

- 1 King 18:46 - And the hand of the LORD was on Elijah; and he girded up his loins, and ran before Ahab to the entrance of Jezreel.
- 2 Kings 3:15 - But now bring me a minstrel. And it came to pass, when the minstrel played, that the hand of the LORD came upon him.

We see that the finger shows power towards judgment and deliverance. The finger is attached to the hand which also signifies power. We see that the hand of God (Holy Spirit) shows not just the power of God working, but also the action of God doing something. In 1 Kings, it shows that Elijah had strength and went forth to do the will of God before Ahab. Also, in 2 Kings, it shows that the hand of God was upon that particular minstrel to do the work/action of God.

Dew – Symbolizes Refreshment, Growth

- Genesis 27:28 - Therefore God give thee of the dew of heaven, and the fatness of the earth, and plenty of corn and wine...
- Isaiah 18:4 - For so the LORD said unto me, I will take my rest, and I will consider in my dwelling place like a clear heat upon herbs, and like a cloud of dew in the heat of harvest.
- Hosea 14:5 - I will be as the dew unto Israel: he shall grow as the lily, and cast forth his roots as Lebanon.

The dew of heaven brings fatness to the Earth. Dew shows the refreshment in our life and what God does for us. We see in Isaiah that they describe it as a 'cloud of dew in the heat of harvest.' Imagine this: on hot day it would be refreshing to see a cloud of dew coming to cool you off. In the same way, the Holy Spirit brings a daily refreshment and growth in our walk with God.

Gift – Symbolizes the Holy Spirit freely given to us by God

- Acts 2:38 - Then Peter said unto them, Repent, and be baptized every one of you in the name of Jesus Christ for the remission of sins, and ye shall receive the gift of the Holy Ghost.

When we think about a gift, it is given freely to us. There is nothing that you or I can do to receive a gift. We are not able to work for it and we cannot buy it; it is given freely through love. The Holy Spirit is given freely for the ones that accept Christ into their lives and they are sealed with it. It is a gift given to us to be fully equipped to fight against the kingdom of the devil and be victorious in this spiritual warfare.

Fire – Symbolizes the Refining/Purifying Power of God

- Isaiah 4:4 - When the Lord shall have washed away the filth of the daughters of Zion, and shall have purged the blood of Jerusalem from the midst thereof by the spirit of judgment, and by the spirit of burning.
- Malachi 3:1-3 - Behold, I will send my messenger, and he shall prepare the way before me: and the LORD, whom ye seek, shall suddenly come to his temple, even the messenger of the covenant, whom ye delight in: behold, he shall come, saith the LORD of hosts. But who may abide the day of his coming? and who shall stand when he appeareth? for he is like a refiner's fire, and like fullers' soap: And he shall sit as a refiner and purifier of silver: and he shall purify the sons of Levi, and purge them as gold and silver, that they may offer unto the LORD an offering in righteousness.
- Acts 2:3 - And there appeared unto them cloven tongues like as of fire, and it sat upon each of them.

I would like to cover this representation in a little bit more detail, since it is a subject that many people today are confused on. Because of this, I would like to tell you that fire is a symbol of refining and purifying power. The next part of this book will be going into detail on the receiving, filling, and baptism of the Holy Spirit and the 'fire' that many refer to when speaking of the Holy Spirit.

Notes

Part 4:
Receiving, Filling & Baptism in the Holy Spirit

In this part I would like to explain the difference between receiving the Holy Spirit, being filled with the Spirit, and being baptized in the Holy Spirit. This is a concept that many people are either confused about or do not understand the differences in those three categories. Others believe that once you repent and accept Christ as your Lord and Savior that you not only receive the Holy Spirit, but you are also filled and baptized at the same time. The Word of God clearly distinguishes the differences of these three subjects. The reason we need to cover the differences is because it is important for us to realize that the Gifts of the Spirit are given, usually, only to the ones that are *baptized*.

Now, out of these gifts there are a couple that can be given without being baptized in the Holy Spirit; this is because of the seven Spirits of the Lord, the other essence of the Spirit.

If you remember, they were the Spirit of the Lord, Spirit of Wisdom, Spirit of Knowledge, Spirit of Understanding, Spirit of Counsel, Spirit of Fear, and the Spirit of Might. Now of the seven essences, two of them are also gifts: Wisdom and Knowledge. These two gifts can manifest without someone being baptized because the Spirit of the Lord and the Spirit of Fear can counsel you into understanding, and by this you receive Wisdom and Understanding. Through the Word of God, you can be guided by the Holy Spirit. Therefore, you can also have the Spirit of Might that gives power to the words you say and what you do.

Now, you may say you've seen some being healed every now and then without someone having the gift of healing - this is possible through faith, but it is different than the actual gift of healings from the Holy Spirit, which we will cover a little later in the gifts of the Holy Spirit. This situation can also apply to some of the other gifts but not all of them.

Receiving

Receiving the Holy Spirit happens when you decide to follow God and give your life to Him – the moment you become a child of God.

- John 3:16 - For God so loved the world, that he gave his only begotten Son, that whosoever believeth in him should not perish, but have everlasting life.
- John 20:22 - And when he had said this, he breathed on them, and saith unto them, Receive ye the Holy Ghost.

- 2 Corinthians 1:22 - Who hath also sealed us, and given the earnest of the Spirit in our hearts.
- 2 Corinthians 5:5 - Now he that hath wrought us for the selfsame thing is God, who also hath given unto us the earnest (means Sealed here) of the Spirit.
- Ephesians 1:13-14 - In whom ye also trusted, after that ye heard the word of truth, the gospel of your salvation: in whom also after that ye believed, ye were sealed with that holy Spirit of promise, which is the earnest of our inheritance until the redemption of the purchased possession, unto the praise of his glory.

As a child of God, you have been sealed with the Spirit of God. In John 3:16, it says that those that believe in Him should not perish but have everlasting life. This everlasting life is what we have because we received the Holy Spirit, and it was sealed on us. Sealing is an indication of receiving. In John 20:22, it speaks about how Jesus Christ breathed on them and said, "receive the Holy Ghost." Breathing is an indication of life that is given, through the receiving of the Holy Ghost. In Ephesians 1, it is written that after we have heard the word of truth, which is the gospel of salvation, and once we have believed, we are sealed with the promise of the Holy Spirit.

To put this simply: the receiving of the Holy Spirit is something that all children of God, that believe and have accepted Him as their Lord and personal Savior, get. This is the first experience we have with the Holy Spirit. The Holy Spirit is what we are sealed with, and at the end of times when Christ comes for His children, this is what raises us up to eternal life with Christ. I would like to clarify: Paul in 1 Corinthians 12:13, talks about that this Spirit is what baptizes us into the body of

Christ. Some read this and assume that if we get baptized in the body, we were baptized in the spirit, but this is not true. This 'baptism' that Paul speaks about here is for when we become part of the family because we have received the Holy Spirit.

Being Filled

Being filled is when you as a child of God start accessing the Spirit of God and allow the Holy Spirit to start working with more power through you for God's work.

- John 4:10 - Jesus answered and said unto her, If thou knewest the gift of God, and who it is that saith to thee, Give me to drink; thou wouldest have asked of him, and he would have given thee living water.
- John 7:37-39 - In the last day, that great day of the feast, Jesus stood and cried, saying, If any man thirst, let him come unto me, and drink. He that believeth on me, as the scripture hath said, out of his belly shall flow rivers of living water. (But this spake he of the Spirit, which they that believe on him should receive: for the Holy Ghost was not yet given; because that Jesus was not yet glorified.)
- Ephesians 5:18 - And be not drunk with wine, wherein is excess; but be filled with the Spirit;
- Acts 2:4a - And they were all filled with the Holy Ghost (this verse speaks about being filled and baptism).
- Acts 4:29-31 – And now, Lord, behold their threatenings: and grant unto thy servants, that with all boldness they may speak thy word, By stretching forth thine hand to heal; and that signs and wonders may be done by the name of thy holy child Jesus. And when they had prayed, the place was shaken where they were assembled together; and they were

all filled with the Holy Ghost, and they spake the word of God with boldness.

- Galatians 5:22-23 - But the fruit of the Spirit is love, joy, peace, longsuffering, gentleness, goodness, faith, Meekness, temperance: against such there is no law.

Being filled in the Spirit is something that all children of God should look for to achieve and then live in. I would like to say that you can be filled in the Spirit of God, and still not be baptized in the Holy Spirit. To be filled in the Spirit you must be looking for it and drinking of it. John 4:10 speaks about having this filling in you.

You must drink from Christ; it must be given to you and you must accept it. Just as in John 7:37-39 it speaks about if any man thirsts - meaning you must desire it, you must crave it, you must thirst for it - and comes to Him and drinks, living water will flow out of his belly. This living water is a power, a joy that comes from the Spirit, that comes over you. Being filled in the Spirit does not just happen once; many believe once you are filled, you are always filled and don't need multiple fillings, but that is not true.

We see in Acts 2, when the apostles were baptized in the Holy Spirit, they were also filled in the Holy Spirit. Later in Acts 4:29-31, we see it again when they prayed all together and were filled with the Holy Ghost and then spoke boldly the Word of God. Being filled means that you are able to take part of the power of the Holy Spirit that was given to you.

Think about it this way: if you fill a water bottle to the top, it's filled. Throughout the day, you take sips to keep yourself hydrated, the water level drops a little. Then something happens and you must run to get somewhere and once you get there you realize you're really thirsty, so now you drink, but not just sips. From three-quarters of a full bottle you're down to one-quarter filled. Before you realize it, even before the day is out, you must REFILL the water bottle again.

It is the same thing with God - you pray, stay in the Word of God, and worship and praise God to become filled so that through the day when you're in the will of God you use this filling to have the power, the courage, and the strength to keep doing the work of God.

If you do not stay filled in the Spirit of the Lord you will leave an opening for the devil to enter and bring you down, and this can lead you astray from God. In Ephesians 5:18, there is a command given, saying not to be filled with wine or drunk, but be filled with the Spirit. This means that this filling is also having the Fruits of the Spirit in you and for them to be visible. Galatians 5 says love, joy, peace, longsuffering, gentleness, goodness, faith, meekness, and temperance are the Fruits of the Spirit. These will be visible in your life once you're filled with the Spirit. Being filled is you surrendering to the Spirit, to allow the Spirit to truly guide and control what you do. One of the best ways to explain being filled by the Spirit is that you have God through the Spirit, and in the baptism God has you.

Baptism in Holy Spirit
This is when the Spirit of God has you, it has full control, you have been immersed in it.

- Mark 16:17 - And these signs shall follow them that believe; In my name shall they cast out devils; they shall speak with new tongues; …

- Luke 24:49 - And, behold, I send the promise of my Father upon you: but tarry ye in the city of Jerusalem, until ye be endued with power from on high.
- Acts 1:5 - For John truly baptized with water; but ye shall be baptized with the Holy Ghost not many days hence.
- Acts 1:8 - But ye shall receive power, after that the Holy Ghost is come upon you: and ye shall be witnesses unto me both in Jerusalem, and in all Judaea, and in Samaria, and unto the uttermost part of the earth.
- Acts 2:4,6 - And they were all filled with the Holy Ghost, and began to speak with other tongues, as the Spirit gave them utterance. 6. Now when this was noised abroad, the multitude came together, and were confounded, because that every man heard them speak in his own language.
- Acts 10: 44-46a (Cornelius vs 23-48) - While Peter yet spake these words, the Holy Ghost fell on all them which heard the word. And they of the circumcision which believed were astonished, as many as came with Peter, because that on the Gentiles also was poured out the gift of the Holy Ghost. For they heard them speak with tongues, and magnify God.
- Acts 14:21-22 - In the law it is written, With men of other tongues and other lips will I speak unto this people; and yet for all that will they not hear me, saith the Lord. Wherefore tongues are for a sign, not to them that believe, but to them that believe not: but prophesying serveth not for them that believe not, but for them which believe.
- Acts 19:6 - And when Paul had laid his hands upon them, the Holy Ghost came on them; and they spake with tongues, and prophesied.

Before we go into the subject of baptism, I would like to explain some misunderstandings that some have about baptism and the filling of the Holy Spirit. These two are not the same thing and cannot be used interchangeably.

Being Spirit-filled is different than being filled by the Spirit. Being Spirit-filled is when someone tries to live in the Spirit's fruits and what the Spirit desires. One way to say it, is that being Spirit-filled is that you have the Holy Spirit and being filled by the Spirit is that the Holy Spirit has you. Because of this, someone may be many times Spirit-filled, because they are always searching for what the Spirit wants and they live in the fruits. Being filled by the Spirit is usually, but not always, someone that is allowing himself or herself to be controlled by the Holy Spirit; this leads many times into the Gifts of Holy Spirit and being empowered to use them. That is why being by the Spirit is usually connected to the ones that are baptized in the Holy Spirit.

This gift of receiving and baptism is for everyone; we find this out in Acts 2:37-39. Acts 1:8 talks about the apostles receiving power and being witnesses (referring to baptism) to Jerusalem, Judea, Samaria, and to the end of the world. Jesus has called us all, just as it says to go and make disciples, teaching all of what He has taught, in Matthew 28:18-20.

In Acts 1:5, even Jesus speaks about being baptized in the Holy Spirit. Even today, scholars do not argue about whether there is a baptism of the Holy Spirit but about whether baptism occurs in our time now or only happened then for Jesus' elected disciples and apostles. The whole Bible is profitable for teaching and, when teaching happens, application should follow from what we have learned.

The first outward sign of being baptized in the Holy Spirit is speaking in tongues and this is where there is a large controversy. Baptism helps us do God's will to the fullest capacity. To be true witnesses for Christ. In Acts 19:1-6, Paul is speaking to the people in Ephesus that have accepted Christ and were baptized by John. He speaks to them knowing that they have received the Holy Spirit but not baptism. In the end, Paul laid his hands on them and the Holy Spirit came upon them (baptism) and they spoke in tongues and prophesized.

In Acts 2:4-6, they were filled (baptism) and spoke in tongues. In Acts 19:6, yet again, they were baptized in the Holy Spirit and spoke in tongues. The phrase "fell upon them," is used as another way of expressing being baptized in the Holy Spirit.

There is a verse that many quote in their argument that speaking in tongues is only to be a witness to the Jews, so that they will know that the Messiah has come. The verse is Isaiah 28:11- 'For with stammering lips and another tongue will he speak to this people.' Paul also uses this verse in 1 Corinthians 14:21-22; he uses it here not only to show that it was fulfilled, but to show that speaking in tongues is a sign of baptism that was visible for all the unbelievers to see the supernatural power of God, for sinners to see an outward sign. We still need this sign today.

In Acts 9:17, when Paul was filled with the Holy Spirit (baptism), many say he didn't speak in tongues, but Paul himself said he spoke more tongues then all (1 Corinthians 14:18). Here the purpose, or primary reason, was to show that Paul had empowerment in his apostolic (mission) ministry.

In addition, Acts 10 records the filling of the Spirit of Cornelius in his home. It says that while Peter yet was still talking that the Holy Ghost fell upon them (baptism), the Gentiles not the Jews. How do we know for sure they were baptized? Verse 46 says they heard them speaking in tongues and magnifying God. And Peter was astonished. This shows that among the gentiles there was speaking of tongues without unbelieving Jews around. Others may say, 'well the apostles were there,' but there was no reason for witnessing to them anymore for they were baptized already and believed.

Did you notice that, throughout the verses used, the only time you heard people prophesying was once they spoke in tongues? The reason being is because baptism is a requirement to prophecy or to have any of the other gifts of the Holy Spirit, other than the few exceptions covered earlier.

Baptism of Fire

- Matthew 3:11 - I indeed baptize you with water unto repentance. but he that cometh after me is mightier than I, whose shoes I am not worthy to bear: he shall baptize you with the Holy Ghost, and with fire...
- Exodus 3:2 - And the angel of the LORD appeared unto him in a flame of fire out of the midst of a bush: and he looked, and, behold, the bush burned with fire, and the bush was not consumed.
- Psalms 104:4 - Who maketh his angels spirits; his ministers a flaming fire...

91

- Isaiah 4:4 - When the Lord shall have washed away the filth of the daughters of Zion, and shall have purged the blood of Jerusalem from the midst thereof by the spirit of judgment, and by the spirit of burning.
- Malaci 3:1-3 - Behold, I will send my messenger, and he shall prepare the way before me: and the LORD, whom ye seek, shall suddenly come to his temple, even the messenger of the covenant, whom ye delight in: behold, he shall come, saith the LORD of hosts. But who may abide the day of his coming? and who shall stand when he appeareth? for he is like a refiner's fire, and like fullers' soap: And he shall sit as a refiner and purifier of silver: and he shall purify the sons of Levi, and purge them as gold and silver, that they may offer unto the LORD an offering in righteousness.
- Acts 2:3 - And there appeared unto them cloven tongues like as of fire, and it sat upon each of them.

This subject is a subject of great confusion in our generation. Today, many people believe that 'fire' speaks about 'judgement.' There are verses in the Bible that do speak of fire that will come down as judgement for specific times or things. But in this passage, this is not what it means. It does not seem to make sense because the passage says you will be *baptized* with the Holy Spirit *and Fire*. This means that this fire is a baptism as well, that the children of God can receive. The apostles received both. In some of the passages above, we see the burning bush or the pillar of fire each of which also show a refined power of God - a bush that does not burn and a pillar of guidance.

In Psalms, we see that it makes the angels spirits: and His ministers a flaming fire, a power that they can use to do the work of ministers. In Isaiah, it speaks about the Spirit of

Judgment and the Spirit of Burning (Fire); it shows that the Spirit of Burning will wash/cleanse the filth and purify Zion and cleanse the bloodstains of Jerusalem. We see here that it is a form of cleaning that which is wrong, of purifying what is there. The baptism of fire is a power that is given to the men of God to cleanse, purify, or refine something or someone.

In addition to this, we see in Malachi that it is written about this fire as a refiner and purifier of silver. We don't think about this, but fire cleanses and purifies. Just as when you put gold through the fire, each time it will become purer. The power of fire is the power to cleanse and remove what must be removed to be made pure in front of God. This is another reason why you hear people say "Holy Spirit Fire" when they cast out a demon, praying for someone that is willing to be cleansed or anyone that has some type of spiritual attachment, whether in addiction, sickness, or spirits.

We use the "Holy Spirit Fire" to be cleansed or purified by God; it is a power to use against the kingdom of the devil. It is evoked to break any chain, break any bondages, break any attachments that have been linked to someone. This fire is a refinement fire, to remove and cleanse someone that has spiritual attachments that are preventing them from moving forward to do the will of God.

There are times when we meet people that have tried every type of medication, every type of therapy to try to be free of addictions like lust, fornication, hatred, or many other sins and no matter what they do, they are not able to break free from whatever they have. The fire of the Holy Spirit is a power that we can be baptized with to break these bondages of spirits of infirmities, demons, addictions, or anything that may have a spiritual attachment. The Fire will remove, cast out, and take out what is necessary for the person to be free from bondages or chains that were attached in the spirit world that many times we can't see, or are aware of, in our life.

Even so, we must not just use the word "fire" in the context of the Holy Spirit, as many do without knowing what it really is. It is a baptism of power that is given to fight against the kingdom of the devil and his army. It is a power for removal, to cleanse and to purify; it does not mean that it will be something comfortable or desirable. To be cleansed can be out of our comfort zone. It is also a power for us to set others free from the bondages that they may have. It is the power that we may be equipped with to be victorious in the spiritual war against the enemy.

Conclusion

Some say that you do not need to speak in tongues to be baptized because Paul states that not all will speak in tongues, others will prophesy. Paul is actually stating here that not all will speak in tongues because receiving the Holy Spirit is different than baptism. This is one reason. The other reason he says this is because he's also referring to speaking in tongues as the interpretation of them, meaning some sort of prophecy in different tongues that needs to be interpreted.

I have experienced this multiple times; on one instance, the prophet was blind, and he would prophecy in tongues while another would interpret, they always travelled together for this purpose. Each time, the prophecy would be right on with what was happening and what needed to be changed in the congregation or in revealing someone's hidden things.

Many have seen false prophets, healers, or made-up tongues and, because of this, they believe it is fake and it no longer exists. Does this mean that because you hear and read many false doctrines, encounter false Christians, false singers, and hear false prayers that you should stop listening to good doctrines, or being a good Christian or singer, or that you should stop praying? No, in fact, this should make you want to grow closer to God and experience Him to the fullest extent to be the light that He has called us to be.

Another reason many don't believe, or say they don't, in the baptism of the Holy Spirit is because it is tough to get to a level or fellowship with Christ to receive the baptism. Many Christians today do not spend much time in prayer or in the Word of God, to study, to speak with God. But they expect to grow with Christ.

A relationship with Christ is just like any other relationship. You speak, God listens, then God speaks, and you listen. A true fellowship requires sacrifice, time, understanding, even pain and suffering on your part and Christ's (when you sin or don't live how you should this is pain and suffering for Christ and no true fellowship hurts someone that loves you so much), and much time to grow. A relationship is 50 percent from you and 50 percent from God. You can't expect to do only ten percent and expect God to give 50 percent. God does His part, you do your part, and this leads to a fifty/fifty, equally split relationship.

The Bible tells of a parable in Matthew 25 that speaks about talents. This parable about the talents shows that if you are responsible for little with what God gives you, being a good and faithful servant, God will give you more. Same thing with the baptism and the Gifts - if you expect to grow with God, you must be responsible with what He gives you first, including building your fellowship with Christ. From there you will grow, and God can give you more. You need to understand that to have the gift of prophecy, healing, miracles, or any of the other gifts is a big responsibility. Until we reach the next level of responsibility, we need to grow in our current responsibility, the Word of God, prayer, holiness, humbleness, humility, and the Fear of the Lord, among others. At that time, just as I wrote previously, you will be filled in the Spirit and have God and God will have you through the baptism.

Notes

Part 5:
Nine Gifts of the
Holy Spirit

We are moving from the seven-fold, or essence, of the Spirit into another area of the Holy Spirit. This area is comprised of the nine Spiritual gifts that as children of God we have access to. These gifts are just as stated in 1 Corinthians 12:4-11: the Gifts of Wisdom, Knowledge, Faith, Healings, Miracles, Prophecy, Discerning of Spirits, Different kind of Tongues, and Interpretation of Tongues. First Corinthians 12:11 says that He as the Holy Spirit will give to the beholder how He sees fit.

These gifts can be broken into three categories: Power, Revealing, and Speaking gifts. Now, we talked previously about the seven-fold of the Holy Spirit and we spoke about Wisdom and Knowledge. Because of this, I will cover these two and another in a short summary of what they are, and more importantly, why out of the nine gifts of the Holy Spirit these two plus one other can be accessed or acquired without being baptized in the Holy Spirit.

The Nine Gifts

1. Wisdom
2. Knowledge
3. Faith
4. Healing
5. Miracles
6. Prophecy
7. Discerning of Spirits
8. Speaking in tongues
9. Interpreting of Tongues

Wisdom and Knowledge

The gift of wisdom that the Holy Spirit gives us is God's Wisdom; simply put, it is what we consider the supernatural intelligence of God's thinking, His creativity, how He puts things together, His thoughts, His Might, and the supremacy of His authority overall. Things that seem hidden or kept secret from us will no longer be kept secret, He will start revealing the truth to us. What we consider the mysteries of God (implied in the often-used phrase "God works in mysterious ways") shall be open to us, revealed to us, through the Spirit of Wisdom and Understanding. The wisdom of God is also including what the Holy Spirit hears the Father speak and then reveals to us.

In addition to this, the gift of Knowledge is the gift that reveals what is good and evil, what is pure and righteous to God the Father. This gift allows us to see how God sees what is good. This can help us become closer to God, by removing what is wrong and evil, what is unclean in our lives, and this will bring us closer to righteousness and holiness in our life. As a child of God myself, this is something even I consistently want to grow in, to become more holy and right in front of God's eyes and remove all that should not be in my life. Knowing what is right from wrong, a person that has wisdom and knowledge will have a positive effect on the children of God. It will give us more light/insight into God the Father which will help us realize who we are. This will help us humble ourselves in humility to know our place in front of God.

Now, earlier I said you can have access to these gifts without being baptized so let's discuss why these two gifts, out of the nine, are able to be received by children of God even without the baptism of the Holy Spirit. If you remember earlier, we said that the Holy Spirit is a seven-fold Spirit. This means that the other folds can be accessed if you have received the Holy Spirit and it can manifest through you. The seven Spirits are Wisdom, Knowledge, Understanding, Counsel, Might, Fear, and the Spirit of the Lord. You may say, well I have heard many preachers and pastors that speak with this type of wisdom and knowledge and you're saying that they are not baptized, how is this possible?

The answer is quite simple. As a child of God we have access through the Holy Spirit - that is why even today we have pastors, preachers, evangelists, and other men of God that, when they speak and preach the word of God, have wisdom (Spirit of Wisdom) and knowledge (Spirit of Knowledge) and understanding (Spirit of Understanding), which come from the Holy Spirit. They are able to counsel (Spirit of Counsel) men and women of God in the right way.

In addition, when they speak, they speak with power, with authority and you can feel that power (Spirit of Might) and the conviction (Spirit of Fear of the Lord) in you when they speak. We need to comprehend that the seven spirits are other essences/folds of the Holy Spirit that can each work separately, but also with one another, since these seven are one. This is what allows us to have access to these two amazing gifts of the Holy Spirit without baptism, because they are also able to work separate from the fold.

Reflect on this: we have many great preachers, pastors, evangelists, and men of God that may have knowledge, wisdom, and power behind their words and messages which come from the Spirit's works, but how many of those people have you seen that are able to achieve or activate the other seven gifts of the Holy Spirit?

You might say, "well, I have seen healings before, doesn't that mean that they have the gift of healing?" But healing once is not the same as the gift of healing, or a miracle, or the speaking or interpreting of tongues or spirit of prophecy. The spirit of prophecy can be an exception, it is accessible through other manifestations of the Holy Spirit by visions and dreams (which must be verified and understood). The Lord speaks and reveals past, present, and future events with dreams and visions through the Holy Spirit which will become a prophetic word or prophesy of the future, present, or past for His people or the world: this comes from the Spirit of Understanding. The other six gifts come through the baptism of the Holy Spirit. That is why many times, in their ministry, you don't hear about healings, miracles, or possibly prophecies, or demons that are cast out, but what you do hear from them and from their followers is about the teaching and wisdom, or the power, that was there and that it provokes people to give their lives to Christ.

I'm not saying that their ministry is not good, as there are still people turning to Christ after hearing the gospel preached to them. What we do need to realize is that they are stopping the rest of the works of the Holy Spirit that could help many thousands, if not tens to hundreds of thousands, through healings, deliverances, and miracles that they need in their lives.

What we need to realize is that God works around us to get His message across - if we have not received the baptism yet, He can give us dreams and visions and through the spirits of understanding, wisdom, and knowledge, we will learn and understand how to interpret these dreams, vision.

Gift of Faith

- 1 Corinthians 2:5 - That your faith should not stand in the wisdom of men, but in the power of God.
- 2 Corinthians 5:7 - For we walk by faith, not by sight...
- Ephesians 2:8 - For by grace are ye saved through faith; and that not of yourselves: it is the gift of God...
- Matthew 21:19-21 - And when he saw a fig tree in the way, he came to it, and found nothing thereon, but leaves only, and said unto it, Let no fruit grow on thee henceforward for ever. And presently the fig tree withered away. And when the disciples saw it, they marvelled, saying, How soon is the fig tree withered away! Jesus answered and said unto them, Verily I say unto you, If ye have faith, and doubt not, ye shall not only do this which is done to the fig tree, but also if ye shall say unto this mountain, Be thou removed, and be thou cast into the sea; it shall be done.

106

- Matthew 14:28-31 - And Peter answered him and said, Lord, if it be thou, bid me come unto thee on the water. And he said, Come. And when Peter was come down out of the ship, he walked on the water, to go to Jesus. But when he saw the wind boisterous, he was afraid; and beginning to sink, he cried, saying, Lord, save me. And immediately Jesus stretched forth his hand, and caught him, and said unto him, O thou of little faith, wherefore didst thou doubt?

- Mark 10:52 - And Jesus said unto him, Go thy way; thy faith hath made thee whole. And immediately he received his sight, and followed Jesus in the way.

- Luke 17:5 - And the apostles said unto the Lord, Increase our faith.

- John 14:12 - Verily, verily, I say unto you, He that believeth on me, the works that I do shall he do also; and greater works than these shall he do; because I go unto my Father.

- James 2:17 - Even so faith, if it hath not works, is dead, being alone.

- Daniel 3:17-18 - If it be so, our God whom we serve is able to deliver us from the burning fiery furnace, and he will deliver us out of thine hand, O king. But if not, be it known unto thee, O king, that we will not serve thy gods, nor worship the golden image which thou hast set up.

To start off, we need to understand that the Gift of Faith through the Holy Spirit is different than the 'saving faith' that we have. In Ephesians 2:8, it speaks about saving faith, the faith that we have through the grace of God towards eternal life. Let's say that this is the simple faith of all believers. Faith in Jesus Christ as the Son of God, the faith just as it says in John 3:16, that if we believe in Him (Jesus Christ) we should not perish but have everlasting life through Him. The faith of trusting in God and not in man. Or, as it says in 2 Corinthians, that we walk by this faith and not through sight.

Overall, the simple faith is the beginning level of faith of the children of God: we know He is the Son of God, He died for our sins, was raised from the grave, and is at the right hand of the Father. The Word of God tells us that we all have a measure of faith. A lot of times we try to ask for healing, for a miracle, from God and we pray for this healing or miracle consistently, but most of the time nothing happens because we do not have enough faith. Other times, God may listen and allow this to happen, which can increase your faith. Increasing your faith is possible just as it says in Luke 17:5, where it tells us that the apostles said to the Lord to increase their faith; this faith can increase through the work of God in your life. For us to have a greater faith, the gift of faith must be given to us.

This gift is given by the Holy Spirit to fulfill God's will for others. In 1 Corinthians 12:7, it tells us that these gifts, including the gift of faith, is for all to profit in the body of Christ. This is the Gift that gives a man or woman incredible faith and belief in the mighty power of God, to do anything and everything.

In Daniel 3, it talks about the faith of Daniel and they three that believed that God could deliver them and that even if He decided not to, they still wouldn't worship the other gods. And they were delivered. Another verse, in Matthew 21, says that Jesus told a fig tree to not produce fruit any longer and it dried up right in front of them; the apostles describe that they were astonished at what they saw.

Jesus responds and says that, if you have faith, you can tell this mountain to move and be cast into the sea and it will happen. Jesus Christ said that we will do even greater works than He, in John 14:12. This is the same faith that Noah had to build the ark when no rain existed before, the faith that Sarah had that she would conceive even in her advanced age. As it says in Matthew 14, Peter had faith to walk on water but then he was afraid and lost his faith and he started to sink, and Jesus' response was to say, 'you of little faith, why did you doubt?'

This Gift of Faith will allow you no doubt. The Gift of Faith is what provides full confidence and assurance, an unshakeable will, without doubt in what Christ has spoken in His promises and Word. If you remember, when we were speaking about the seven Spirits of the Lord, I was saying that the Spirit of the Fear of the Lord was the master key to the other Spirits. In this same way, the Gift of Faith is the master key that allows the other gifts to come forth as well.

This faith is the faith that even when faced with an obstacle, a problem, or a situation as big as the world, you have no doubt; you know it is possible to conquer even if you have to move a mountain by faith or bring people back from death - this is the true power of the Gift of Faith. This faith will lift the congregation of God, if will edify it. The men and women of God that have this Gift of Faith, you know that they fully depend on God, for they know that God has all the might to do what has been written, and because of this he, or she, is usually humble, filled with humility, but at the same time is fearless in the will and plan of God, filled with zealousness for God. These men and women know and understand their place with God and the will that God has called them to accomplish. Even if the will of God takes them to the most perilous and hazardous places to go, they will go filled with faith.

Gift of Healing

- James 5:15-16 – And the prayer of faith shall save the sick, and the Lord shall raise him up; and if he have committed sins, they shall be forgiven him. Confess your faults one to another, and pray one for another, that ye may be healed. The effectual fervent prayer of a righteous man availeth much.
- Matthew 4:23-24 - And Jesus went about all Galilee, teaching in their synagogues, and preaching the gospel of the kingdom, and healing all manner of sickness and all manner of disease among the people. And his fame went throughout all Syria: and they brought unto him all sick people that were taken with divers diseases and torments, and those which were possessed with devils, and those which were lunatic, and those that had the palsy; and he healed them.
- Mark 1:30-34 - But Simon's wife's mother lay sick of a fever, and anon they tell him of her. And he came and took her by the hand, and lifted her up; and immediately the fever left her, and she ministered unto them. And at even, when the sun did set, they brought unto him all that were diseased, and them that were possessed with devils. And all the city was gathered together at the door, And he healed many that were sick of divers diseases, and cast out many devils; and suffered not the devils to speak, because they knew him.
- Acts 8:7 – For unclean spirits, crying with loud voice, came out of many that were possessed with them: and many taken with palsies, and that were lame, were healed.

- Acts 9:33-34 - And there he found a certain man named Aeneas, which had kept his bed eight years, and was sick of the palsy. And Peter said unto him, Aeneas, Jesus Christ maketh thee whole: arise, and make thy bed. And he arose immediately.
- Acts 28:9 - So when this was done, others also, which had diseases in the island, came, and were healed...

Earlier, I was speaking about how the gift of healing that is given by the Holy Spirit is different than just a one-time healing. In the book of James, chapter 5, it speaks about how through faith and prayer and forgiving, praying for one another, there can be healing done. You may have heard, just as I have heard, of stories where someone would be praying for a healing done in their life, and God granting their prayer. This is the prayer of faith and the fervent prayer that James speaks about. A prayer when, through your belief/faith in God, He, through His grace and mercy, decided to heal you.

Look at it in this way. A child might do everything according to his duty, or what we call "chores," and even after this the son or daughter may ask the parents to give him/her a gift, or their favorite type of food, or to go out. Now, the father or mother may give them what they want not because they deserve it, not because they did more than required, but because the mother or father has compassion, mercy, and grace for their child. This is how this type of healing works, the healing of faith. We do what we are required - in Luke 17:10 it says that even after we have done all we have been commanded by God, all we can say in the end is that we have only done our duty. This verse shows us that if God decided to heal us when we asked, it was only because He decided to show His mercy and grace towards us.

Furthermore, the gift of healing is different in the way that it doesn't require a fervent prayer, it is only given because of God's mercy for us. Now, the difficult part is that this Gift is closely related to the Gift of Faith and Miracles. The reason it is close to faith is because, as we spoke earlier, the Gift of Faith is a greater faith of having full confidence and unshakeable faith that what God has spoken, what is in His Word and His promises, it will come to pass. Because of this, the Gift of Faith is a requirement of knowing that healing is possible.

In Matthew 4, it says that Jesus went through all of Galilee and through the synagogues preaching, but not just that, He was healing all manner of sickness and disease - He healed them all. Mark 1 speaks about Simon's mother-in-law, that she had a fever that wouldn't leave but when He laid His hand on her, she got up immediately and the fever left her. Later on, in this same passage, it says that when evening came, many that were sick and diseased among them came and were healed. Acts 8:7 says that people with demon possessions and those that were lamed where healed. In Acts 9, there was a man, Aeneas, that had been sick for eight years with palsy and then he rose up immediately when he was healed by Peter. Another verse in Acts 28 shows again that many more where healed.

I wrote all these for you to see that the Gift of Healing can be applied to many people, and that person that has received this gift is able to heal anyone in the name of Jesus Christ, in His will and timing. When you think about your life, or just in general, ask yourself how many times have you heard this happen, how many times have you seen this happen?

Here is the what we need to understand: this gift is attached to the Gift of Faith, but also to the Spirit of Understanding so that we can see God's will in the situation of healing. For when we heal with this gift, we need to heal according to God's will. With this Gift there comes responsibility as well; when anyone comes to be healed, we need to ask God if it His will for healing (unless He has given you the revelation or understanding that it is) to happen and, if so, you have been given the Gift and authority by God to heal instantly. When you receive this gift, you are able to not just heal one time, but, based on the grace of God and through His mercy, you will be able to heal multiple times as needed, for you will have been given the authority to do so. You might be asking, "well, why wouldn't God want a healing to happen?"

When we asked our Lord to be our personal savior and for Him to enter into our life and be our master, one phrase we always forget, after we say it, is, "I will follow You for the rest of my days, do what is necessary for me to be saved, for my salvation to be assured forever." When you say this, you have given permission for our Lord and God (Master, Savior) to allow things or put what is necessary in your life to make sure that you will always be saved.

You might not understand that money, cars, houses, or even good health can, and many times will, make you depart from the living God. This then causes a problem; if God allows you to continue, you will lose your salvation. Just as it says in

Hebrews 3:12 – "take heed that none of you have an evil heart of unbelief in departing from God."

You may not see that if you are in good health or have money that this can bring you into having an evil heart, and it will make you depart. And because of this our living Father in heaven, through His mercy and grace, allows situations and problems in our lives that make us stay dependent on Him and realize that we need Him. This then allows us to keep our salvation. For example, we have it written in the Word of God about Paul and his thorn; this thorn was left for him to not become proud of himself, which could lead to many other things, including leading him away from God - just as Lucifer did, due to pride.

God's plan is many times difficult for us to understand, but this doesn't mean that there isn't a plan that is good, just at it says in Roman 8:28 - all works, all that happens is for the good of those that love God; this includes bad and good, sickness and health.

Gift of Miracles

- John 2:9 - When the ruler of the feast had tasted the water that was made wine, and knew not whence it was: (but the servants which drew the water knew;) the governor of the feast called the bridegroom...
- Mark 4:39-41 - And he arose, and rebuked the wind, and said unto the sea, Peace, be still. And the wind ceased, and there was a great calm. And he said unto them, Why are ye so fearful? how is it that ye have no faith? And they feared exceedingly, and said one to another, What manner of man is this, that even the wind and the sea obey him?

- John 6:1-15 (Feeding of the 5000 +)
- John 6:16-27 - So when they had rowed about five and twenty or thirty furlongs, they see Jesus walking on the sea, and drawing nigh unto the ship: and they were afraid.
- John 11:43-44 - And when he thus had spoken, he cried with a loud voice, Lazarus, come forth. And he that was dead came forth, bound hand and foot with graveclothes: and his face was bound about with a napkin. Jesus saith unto them, Loose him, and let him go.
- Matthew 21:19 - And when he saw a fig tree in the way, he came to it, and found nothing thereon, but leaves only, and said unto it, Let no fruit grow on thee henceforward for ever. And presently the fig tree withered away.
- Acts 20:10 - And there sat in a window a certain young man named Eutychus, being fallen into a deep sleep: and as Paul was long preaching, he sunk down with sleep, and fell down from the third loft, and was taken up dead. And Paul went down, and fell on him, and embracing him said, Trouble not yourselves; for his life is in him.
- Acts 6:8 - And Stephen, full of faith and power, did great wonders and miracles among the people.
- Acts 9:40 - But Peter put them all forth, and kneeled down, and prayed; and turning him to the body said, Tabitha, arise. And she opened her eyes: and when she saw Peter, she sat up.

If you remember, the Gift of Faith is also the key that permits you and I to have access to or to bring forth the Gift of Miracles in our life. The Gift of Miracles is different than the Gift of Healing. We usually say, "it was a miracle!" many times when someone is healed of cancer, or when someone is healed of a disease, or a strong type of infection, but these are not miracles, these are healings. Healing is referred to as internal or external sickness or disease of any type that is healed back to optimal health. Miracles/wonders and healings are usually used interchangeably but not always correctly.

A miracle is defined as something that happens that is not comprehensible, an event that does not happen normally. It is not normal and goes against, what we call, scientific law. For example, I knew someone that had an extreme car accident - the car rolled and rolled before coming to a stop. The man came out of the car without one scratch on him, yet the car was broken from one end to another, destroyed. Another example is that in a country in Europe, a man prophesying in a very crowded church for different individuals and, while he was prophesying, the man was hovering in the air above, around 8 to 10 feet, to be able to go from one end to another of the church.

My grandfather one morning went out and found a plant that didn't produce anything and he, in his faith, said to the plant that it should no longer produce and to dry up completely. Within that day, the plant completely dried up and snapped as if it had been dead for days. You might be reading this and thinking to yourself that this story may sound familiar, and that is because it also happened in Matthew 21:19.

In Matthew 21:19 Jesus did this miracle as well; it says that He told the fig tree not to produce and, in that moment, the apostles saw that fig tree wither away in front of their eyes. They were astonished, and Jesus responded and said that if you have faith you can say to a mountain to be moved and be cast into the sea and it will be done. Now this verse can be used either literally or as a comparison to a mountain (problem) in your life. When you think about it, if this is a mountain in your life then, yes, it may require a miracle to move it and cast it aside.

The Gift of Miracles will put people in a state of awe and amazement. Many times, when we think of a miracle, we think of Jesus' first miracle, done at the wedding in John 2:9; it speaks about how Jesus turned water into wine, but not just any type of wine, the best wine. This is considered a miracle.

In addition, Mark 39:41 is another amazing passage. They were on a boat and a strong storm and waves were hitting against their boat and the apostles were afraid, thinking they would perish if nothing changed. They stood up and woke up Jesus, the master, and said, "do you not care if we perish?" He stood up and rebuked the wind and the wind became still and calm, at peace, and yet again they were afraid saying that even the wind listens to Him. The Gift of Miracles is what is considered, in a way, being able to surpass the laws of nature.

In the passage of John 6 is another wonderful miracle - the feeding of the five thousand. The disciples and Jesus were at a mountain and the Passover feast was near. There was a boy who had five loaves of bread and two fishes and they were to be split among thousands that had come to hear Jesus preach and hadn't eaten all day. Jesus told them to sit down and He prayed for the bread and the fish and the disciples dispersed the fish and bread among all the people there, and all of them were filled that were there. What a magnificent miracle that was performed. A miracle because we know that no matter what you try to do in the natural realm to feed five thousand men, plus women and kids, with five loaves and two fishes, it's just not possible.

This miracle, just as the others, shatters the natural realm as if it doesn't even exist. John 6 also has the passage of Jesus walking on water and Peter asking that if it is the Lord to call him out to walk on water too. We see here that Peter was able to walk on water, but then lost his faith and started sinking, and yet again we see here how important faith is, to be able do to miracles as well as healings.

In John 11 (Lazarus) and Acts 9 (Tabitha), Lazarus and Tabitha were dead and then raised back to life. A miracle, as I said, is something the natural realm, or what men believe is impossible, is made possible, because with God all things are possible. Just how God performed miracles through Elijah and Moses.

The Gift of Miracles works within the bounds of the faith you have. This faith can bring miracles to the supernatural realm and perform miraculous wonders. These miracles will uplift and encourage the men and women of our Lord and bring life and joy among the congregation of God. They will bring light and glory upon God for Him to show others that through Him all is possible, that all is reachable with Him, and nothing can hinder His mighty power.

Gift of Prophecy

- Ephesians 4:11-12 - And he gave some, apostles; and some, prophets; and some, evangelists; and some, pastors and teachers; For the perfecting of the saints, for the work of the ministry, for the edifying of the body of Christ…
- Romans 11:29 - For the gifts and calling of God are without repentance.

- 1 Corinthians 13:8-10 - Charity never faileth: but whether there be prophecies, they shall fail; whether there be tongues, they shall cease; whether there be knowledge, it shall vanish away. For we know in part, and we prophesy in part. But when that which is perfect is come, then that which is in part shall be done away.
- 1 Corinthians 14:1-5 - Follow after charity, and desire spiritual gifts, but rather that ye may prophesy. For he that speaketh in an unknown tongue speaketh not unto men, but unto God: for no man understandeth him; howbeit in the spirit he speaketh mysteries. But he that prophesieth speaketh unto men to edification, and exhortation, and comfort. He that speaketh in an unknown tongue edifieth himself; but he that prophesieth edifieth the church. I would that ye all spake with tongues but rather that ye prophesied: for greater is he that prophesieth than he that speaketh with tongues, except he interpret, that the church may receive edifying.
- 1 Corinthians 14:24-25 - But if all prophesy, and there come in one that believeth not, or one unlearned, he is convinced of all, he is judged of all: And thus are the secrets of his heart made manifest; and so falling down on his face he will worship God, and report that God is in you of a truth.
- 1 Corinthians 14:39 - Wherefore, brethren, covet to prophesy, and forbid not to speak with tongues.
- 1 Peter 1:20-21 - Knowing this first, that no prophecy of the scripture is of any private interpretation. For the prophecy came not in old time by the will of man: but holy men of God spake as they were moved by the Holy Ghost.

Before moving forward, we need to understand that God has three ways of using someone in prophecy. The first way is being anointed for a specific purpose and a specific time to accomplish God's will; He is capable to do this because of God's sovereignty. The second is through the gift of Prophecy and a true calling of becoming a prophet (Romans 11:29 shows us that a gift and calling will never be irrevocable or taken away from the one that has given it, but the anointing can be).

Now, in all three of these categories you will prophecy. I would like to first say that prophecy is not what many people believe it is today. One Corinthians 14, verse 3 and 4, say that he who prophesies speaks for edification, exhortation, and comfort. In today's generation you hear someone preaching on a specific subject and, because he or she encouraged or edified you or comforted you, many will say he prophesied today, but this is not so. When someone speaks about something that was on your mind and you receive comfort or edification or encouragement this does not mean it is a prophecy but it is an understanding, a wisdom that has been given to you through the man.

The word prophecy means prediction: a forecast of what will come to pass, what has been, and is to come. It is a revelation, an insight, that is given direct and clear with prophetic word speaking to you from the Holy Spirit. A prophecy usually has a cause and effect and a cause again; this is what I mean: the reason why the Lord God is speaking to you is to tell you what will happen if you continue on your path, if you do not repent or change, and what will happen if you decide to change and the blessings that will follow.

Further on, we will speak about the Gift of Prophecy and because of this we will speak specifically about this gift and its function. Before we move on, we need to define edification, exhortation, and comfort. The reason we need to define these is because in today's generation we speak about these and we believe that a prophecy can only be directed towards happiness and joy, but this is not always the case.

- Edification = a way of instruction or teaching for someone's development towards a personal morality, standards, and intellect of what is logical and rational to them.
- Exhortation = a way of addressing or speaking to someone insistently, urging them to do something, to take action on something, in their life.
- Comfort = state of being free, physical ease, having no pain or worries of a situation or problem in life.

The reason we need to know what they mean is that if we don't understand them truly, we will hear a prophecy in our life and not listen to it because it may be hard to hear or will convict us, and because of this we will take it in the way that it was a false prophecy and not from God.

Ephesians 4:11-12 talks about what we call the five-fold ministry; that our God has called some of us to be apostles, pastors, prophets, evangelists, and teachers. Many people today do not believe in prophets yet here we have evidence that all of them exist. What many people today do is remove prophets from the five-fold ministry and only believe in the rest of God's appointed services. We are not able to remove what is in Scripture just to benefit ourselves - we must take it all and understand that it may not always be what we want to believe.

121

Scripture tells us that these five positions were given for the work of ministry and for the edification of the body of Christ.

If we read in 1 Corinthians 13:8-10, it talks about how speaking in tongues will cease, prophesying will end, and knowledge will end. This is one of the few verses that cessationists (a Protestant section of peoples that believe gifts such as speaking in tongues and prophecy ceased with the Apostolic Age) use today, to say that prophecy doesn't exist anymore. But what they don't understand is they take this verse out of context; when reading the full context, it says that all of this will cease *once that which is perfect has come*. We know that 'perfect' will only happen once we are with Christ, indicating that knowledge of good and evil, speaking in other tongues, and prophecy will not come to an end until we are with Christ for eternity.

If we continue, in 1 Corinthians 14:24-25 it speaks about that if we were all to prophesy that when an unbeliever, or someone that is not learned, would hear, by prophecy he or she will be convicted. One part of a prophecy is for the unbelievers and the unlearned to be convicted when they hear it. How can you be convicted unless there is something that has been revealed in your life from the past and the present? Conviction means you know what has been said is true and it makes you want to turn from your wrong ways to the truth.

The same passage talks about that they will be judged, indicating when they feel this conviction in them, they feel they have been judged of what is wrong and they will turn from their ways. It continues in the passage, saying that the hidden secrets of their hearts will be drawn out, meaning that what we have tried to hide and keep secret from all - whatever type of addiction, lust, or desire - will come to light and will be visible. The passage further says that by this revelation of their life that the person shall fall on their face and worship God for they know that God is truly there and what has been brought to light is true.

The Gift of Prophecy is another exception to baptism of the Holy Spirit because God can work with His children using dreams and visions to reveal to us His plans. This a powerful gift for the men and women of God to have in their life. Paul says, I wish that all would prophecy for prophesying brings conviction, judgment, and reveals secrets that are within. This makes the people vulnerable, to understand that there is a God, a God that has created all, that loves them enough to come and speak to them, to urge them to repentance, to turn from their ways and come back to the living God.

In 1 Corinthians 14:39, Paul further continues and says that we should covet (hunger for, desire, crave) prophecy, to have this gift. In 1 Peter 1:20-21, it reveals that when someone is prophesying, that it does not come from man, but comes from how the Holy Spirit moves them and speaks. If the Spirit moves them this means that they are under the Spirit's control; you cannot move unless the Spirit moves you, indicating full surrender to the Spirit in everything you do.

If you ever wonder why churches die and dwindle in the number of members, or that churches of God seem like they are just like the world (same addictions, desires, lusts), it is because this gift is not present. The gift of prophecy can be given to pastors as well evangelists; it can be given to anyone acting in the five-fold ministry, it is a gift given to build the body of

123

Christ. When you're not able to tell men and women of God apart from men and women of the world, it is because true conviction and judgement is missing in their lives and what they have kept secret is still hidden.

We must pray earnestly and desire the gift of prophecy to be able to make a true transformation in churches today, to bring that light and salt back to the world. We were called to this light and salt, to change the world, to make people desire God, but instead we are the other way, where others do not want us near them. Just as it is written, let us earnestly desire and pray for all to receive the Gift of Prophecy.

Discerning of Spirits

- Matthew 16:15-17 - He saith unto them, But whom say ye that I am? And Simon Peter answered and said, Thou art the Christ, the Son of the living God. And Jesus answered and said unto him, Blessed art thou, Simon Barjona: for flesh and blood hath not revealed it unto thee, but my Father which is in heaven.
- Matthew 24:11,23 - And many false prophets shall rise, and shall deceive many... 23. For there shall arise false Christs, and false prophets, and shall shew great signs and wonders; insomuch that, if it were possible, they shall deceive the very elect.
- 1 John 4:1-3 - Beloved, believe not every spirit, but try the spirits whether they are of God: because many false prophets are gone out into the world. Hereby know ye the Spirit of God: Every spirit that confesseth that Jesus Christ is come in the flesh is of God: And every spirit that confesseth not that Jesus Christ is come in the flesh is not of God: and this is

that [spirit] of antichrist, whereof ye have heard that it should come; and even now already is it in the world.

- Galatians 5:22 - But the fruit of the Spirit is love, joy, peace, longsuffering, gentleness, goodness, faith,

- 1 Corinthians 2:14 - But the natural man receiveth not the things of the Spirit of God: for they are foolishness unto him: neither can he know them, because they are spiritually discerned.

- Colossians 2:8 - Beware lest any man spoil you through philosophy and vain deceit, after the tradition of men, after the rudiments of the world, and not after Christ.

- 1 Timothy 4:1 - Now the Spirit speaketh expressly, that in the latter times some shall depart from the faith, giving heed to seducing spirits, and doctrines of devils; ...

- 2 Corinthians 11:13-15 - For such are false apostles, deceitful workers, transforming themselves into the apostles of Christ. And no marvel; for Satan himself is transformed into an angel of light. Therefore, it is no great thing if his ministers also be transformed as the ministers of righteousness; whose end shall be according to their works.

- John 14:26 - But when the Comforter is come, whom I will send unto you from the Father, even the Spirit of truth, which proceedeth from the Father, he shall testify of me...

I would say this is another truly important gift to have. In the life of a child of God we go through many ups and downs. We hear many teachings and doctrines out there. We run into many people that have powers to do miracles and wonders that we may not understand but are impressed by and, because of this, we follow them believing that what they are saying and doing is the truth. We have family members and friends going

125

from right to left saying this is truth or this is truth. Throughout our lives, if we allow ourselves to be dragged along, we will not understand what is true and right. The Gift of Discerning of Spirits is a gift that can be given to us. Now, all children of God have a measure of discernment of what is good and evil, what is from God and what is not, but this Gift goes beyond that.

The Holy Spirit which lives in us teaches us the truth; it can testify of Christ that He is Lord, that He came on Earth as flesh. In John 14:26, it says that when the Holy Spirit, the comforter, comes that is sent by the Father it is the Spirit of Truth, which comes out of the Father and He will testify of Christ. In Matthew 16:15-17, Jesus ask His apostles who He is. Simeon Peter responds and says that He is Jesus Christ, the Son of God. At his answer, Jesus responds and says that not blood and flesh revealed this to them but the Father.

The Father lives through us in the Holy Spirit which will reveal the truth to us. Galatians 5:22 speaks about the fruits of the spirit, that we need to live a spirit-filled life and produce fruits, for with these fruits and through works we will be able to discern who is of God and who is not.

We may ask ourselves why is this, why would people follow them? The answer is in two different passages, the first from Colossians 2:8: be cautious that no person will indulge you through their philosophy and viewpoint, and in vain deceit, and through the tradition of man and of this world, to take you from Christ.

The second passage is in 1 Corinthians 2:14: it says that natural man believes the truth is foolish, the things of God are foolish in front their eyes. There are people that say they love

God and they are forever saved, because at one point in their life they came before an altar or were baptized in water. The thing is, these people may have done this, but they do not follow in Jesus' footsteps, live in the Spirit, or search God fully and because of this they are lost in the world and easily persuaded towards other directions with not much effort on the part of the persuader. With the power they have and the wonders that they are able to accomplish, the enemy, which is the Devil and his followers, can persuade you in that direction and trick you away from the truth through your own indulgency and curiosity. Even the elite will be persuaded and won over to the devil's side if they're not cautious.

Matthew 24:11,23 talks about that many false prophets will rise. What we need to worry about is that these false prophets will have power to do miracles, wonders, and healings. And it says that many will be deceived and follow them, even the elect. This means that even strong men of God, the elect, will be so deceived, so filled with awe of what they will do, that they will even follow the false prophets. In 2 Corinthians 11:13-15, it says that even the devil himself will dress as an angel of light and, if he does, his followers can too. This alone makes it difficult to discern the 'light' of the devil and the true light of God, that is why even the elect will be fooled by him. In our generation there are very few people that read the Word of God and are filled with the Holy Spirit and because of this many fall from the True Light of God into the false light of the devil.

In 1 Timothy 4:1, it says that many will depart from the true faith and light of God because of seducing, enticing spirits, and doctrines of devils/demons. This indicates that they will have what you might desire, what you want to have because they

127

are seducing you with your desires and wants. We need to replace the flesh's desires and wants with God's desires, otherwise we will be enticed by these spirits and demons. This is the reason why we need this specific gift in the body of Christ. To be able to discern which is the spirit of the antichrist (Devil, Spirits, demons) and which is the and Spirit of God.

In 1 John 4:1-3 it tells us how we can discern the Spirit of God from the Spirit of the Antichrist. It tells us not to believe all the spirits and that we must test the spirits. The Spirit that confesses that 'Jesus Christ has come in flesh,' that is the Spirit of God, but he or she that cannot confess with his/her mouth that Jesus Christ has come in flesh is not of God (this Spirit is the Antichrist). We need to understand this Gift of Discernment of Spirits is important, it opens the door to us to reveal the truth of the Spirit. It reveals which type of spirit is behind the action, behind the desire, if it's the spirit of lust, riches, sex, fornication, homosexuality, hatred, unforgiveness or the many others, the list can go on and on. This is a Gift that reveals the source behind the spirit, or even better put, brings the spotlight right on the spirit to know if it is from God or not.

Different Kinds of Tongues

- Mark 16:14-17- Afterward he appeared unto the eleven as they sat at meat, and upbraided them with their unbelief and hardness of heart, because they believed not them which had seen him after he was risen. [15]And he said unto them, Go ye into all the world, and preach the gospel to every creature. [16]He that believeth and is baptized shall be saved; but he that believeth not shall be damned. And these signs shall follow them that believe; In my name shall they cast out devils; they shall speak with new tongues…

128

- Acts 2:4 - And they were all filled with the Holy Ghost, and began to speak with other tongues, as the Spirit gave them utterance.
- Acts 10:46a - For they heard them speak with tongues, and magnify God.
- Acts 19:6 - And when Paul had laid hands upon them, the Holy Ghost came on them; and they spake with tongues, and prophesied.
- 1 Corinthians 13:13 - Though I speak with the tongues of men and of angels, and have not charity, I am become sounding brass, or a tinkling cymbal.
- 1 Corinthians 14:2,4,5 - For he that speaketh in an unknown tongue speaketh not unto men, but unto God: for no man understandeth him; howbeit in the spirit he speaketh mysteries. He that speaketh in an unknown tongue edifieth himself; but he that prophesieth edifieth the church. I would that ye all spake with tongues but rather that ye prophesied: for greater is he that prophesieth than he that speaketh with tongues, except he interpret, that the church may receive edifying.
- 1 Corinthians 14:4 - He that speaketh in an unknown tongue edifieth himself; but he that prophesieth edifieth the church.
- 1 Corinthians 14:22 - Wherefore tongues are for a sign, not to them that believe, but to them that believe not: but prophesying not for them that believe not, but for them which believe.
- 1 Corinthians 14:39 - Wherefore, brethren, covet to prophesy, and forbid not to speak with tongues.

In a previous section, we covered receiving, being filled, and baptism of the Holy Spirit, and it was covered that speaking in tongues is sign of the baptism of the Holy Spirit. Paul himself writes that speaking in a new tongue is a sign of the baptism of the Holy Spirit, and Jesus said in Mark 16:14-17 that this is the 'great commission,' and told them to go into all the world and all who will receive and be baptized in water shall be saved. But He was not speaking of the baptism of the Holy Spirit, as many teach today. He said that the sign that will follow after being saved and baptized will be casting out of demons and speaking with new tongues. We have here a confirmation from Christ Himself that speaking in tongues comes after, not during, the water baptism. Let's discuss further what speaking in tongues is and its function for a believer.

Acts 2:4, 10:46, and 19:6 are a few of the passages that speak about men being baptized in the Spirit of God (Holy Spirit) and speaking in new tongues. In 1 Corinthians 14:2,4 it says that speaking in tongues, as much as it is a sign of baptism towards unbelievers, is not actually speaking to men, but speaking directly to God, the Father Himself.

At the same time we speak to the Father, we also edify ourselves. If you remember, edification is that you are receiving instruction of what is morally correct and intellectual from God. It is communication between you and the Father in other tongues. Now, these tongues can either be man's tongues or angelic tongues. In 1 Corinthians 13:13, Paul says that he speaks both; he speaks tongues of man as well as angel tongues.

Speaking in tongues is a way of growth, a way of building a stronger fellowship with the living God, our Father in heaven. It is a way for us to find out mysteries, just as it says in 1

130

Corinthians 14:2 that speaking in tongues not only edifies you, but it is the spoken mysteries of God.

When you communicate with God the Father in tongues, you learn, you are instructed in the right way to go. This is why, many children of God that consistently speak in this way with the Father grow and seem as if they understand more. During this communication, you find out the mysteries of God. If you remember, earlier, we were speaking about the Wisdom and Knowledge that the seven Spirits of God can give which are also two of the gifts the Holy Spirit can give to believers. The mysteries of God are considered God's supernatural wisdom and intellect and you receive it during this time of communication with Him. Paul says that he wishes all would speak in tongues and, even more so, to prophecy.

Paul says this because while, yes, speaking in tongues edifies you it does not the church, so he says 'even more so to prophecy,' because prophesying will edify, exhort, and comfort the whole congregation of God. It will instruct us, it will rebuke us for what we might be doing wrong as children of God, it will teach us what is right from wrong in God's moral standards, and we will be comforted knowing that God the Father is with us. It will make the men and women grow spiritually and expand God's kingdom on Earth until His return. In the end, Paul still states that we should not forbid speaking in tongues, he is saying, yes, prophesying is important, but we should not stop speaking in tongues for this also allows an individual, a believer, to grow and have a true fellowship with the Father and to know His mysteries.

Interpretation of Tongues

- 1 Corinthians 14:2,4,5 - For he that speaketh in an unknown tongue speaketh not unto men, but unto God: for no man understandeth him; howbeit in the spirit he speaketh mysteries. He that speaketh in an unknown tongue edifieth himself; but he that prophesieth edifieth the church. I would that ye all spake with tongues but rather that ye prophesied: for greater is he that prophesieth than he that speaketh with tongues, except he interpret, that the church may receive edifying.
- 1 Corinthians 14:13-14 - Wherefore let him that speaketh in an unknown tongue pray that he may interpret. For if I pray in an unknown tongue, my spirit prayeth, but my understanding is unfruitful.
- 1 Corinthians 14:27-28 - If any man speak in an unknown tongue, let it be by two, or at the most by three, and that by course; and let one interpret. But if there be no interpreter, let him keep silence in the church; and let him speak to himself, and to God.

Out of the nine gifts of the Holy Spirit, I would say that this is one of the easiest ones to understand, or at least should be. It is just as it is written: Interpretation of Tongues. For example, if someone comes from a different country, with a different tongue/language, you may either interpret for them, if you know his or her language, or you get someone to interpret on your behalf. It is the same way with the Holy Spirit; you can say that the Holy Spirit is the key to interpreting if someone speaks a different tongue, because He (Holy Spirit) will give you wisdom and understanding to be able to communicate what that person is saying to others.

Most of the time, the reason for the speaking other tongues in public is for a prophecy that is spoken to the church for edification. This language can either be man's language or a language of angels that you or someone else may be speaking, and through the Holy Ghost, it is interpreted for a proper usage in the congregation of God.

Paul, in 1 Corinthians 14, says that speaking in tongues edifies someone and he who prophesied edifies the church. Paul also says that when someone speaks in a different tongue that he should only speak a few words at a time and let someone interpret, but if no one is there that has this gift of interpretation, it is better for the person to be silent and to pray between himself and the Father and this will bring edification to themselves. For, in the same chapter, he says that if no one can interpret, then the one speaking in tongues is unfruitful; it will bring no fruit to bear and will not further understanding to the congregation, even if the Spirit prays.

We, as men and women of God, need to start looking and growing in Christ. It is time for us to start sacrificing our time and to start growing in Christ, in the gifts of the Holy Spirit. If we do this, we will see a strong pouring out of the Holy Spirit among God's children and a mighty power that will come from the church. A power that is fully controlled by the Spirit of God, for God's children have decided to fully surrender themselves for the works of God and will be followed by miracles, wondrous healings, and prophecy from God's children and His Glory will shine everywhere.

Notes

Part 6:
Ministry of the
Holy Spirit

Up to now, we have covered the seven-fold, or essence, of the Spirits, which are called the Seven Spirits of the Lord. We have covered receiving the Holy Spirit, being filled in the Spirit, and baptism of the Spirit, and now we have to discuss the nine gifts of the Holy Spirit. Let's direct our attention to what the Holy Spirit does for us and can do through us. Some of what we will cover here may reflect a little of what we have spoken about earlier as well.

Holy Spirit the Guider

- John 16:13 - Howbeit when he, the Spirit of truth, is come, he will guide you into all truth: for he shall not speak of himself; but whatsoever he shall hear, that shall he speak: and he will shew you things to come.
- Matthew 4:1 - Then was Jesus led up of the Spirit into the wilderness to be tempted of the devil.

- Acts 8:29 - Then the Spirit said unto Philip, Go near, and join thyself to this chariot.
- Acts 13:2 - As they ministered to the Lord, and fasted, the Holy Ghost said, Separate me Barnabas and Saul for the work whereunto I have called them.
- Acts 20:22 - And now, behold, I go bound in the spirit unto Jerusalem, not knowing the things that shall befall me there:
- Romans 8:14 - For as many as are led by the Spirit of God, they are the sons of God.
- Galatians 5:18 - But if ye be led of the Spirit, ye are not under the law.
- Galatians 5:25 - If we live in the Spirit, let us also walk in the Spirit.

When we are confused in the direction that we are supposed to go, the Holy Spirit will guide us. Guiding is to advise or direct the way, just as a conductor or pilot, or even like an usher. It is someone that leads you to where you need to go. Just like a waiter or waitress does - he or she will guide you through the restaurant to were you need to be seated. This is what the Holy Spirit does for us; it will guide us into the direction we must go. This direction may not be always understood by us, why or where we must go somewhere, just as Philip and the Eunuch.

In Galatians 5:25, it says that if we live in the Spirit that we must also walk in the Spirit. This verse then takes us to Galatians 5:18 which says that if we are walking (led, guided) in the Spirit, we are not under the law. What it is saying here is that, if you are led by the Spirit, you will produce the fruits of the Spirit, as the fruits have no law against them (Galatians 5:23). He will guide you to the truth of Christ, which is another reason why He was sent. In Matthew 4:1, it says that Jesus was led up by the Spirit into the wilderness to be tempted. You may say, "why would the Spirit lead you where you will be tested into temptation?"

Let me tell you something: in life, we are guided in many situations for testing our faith. Jesus was led there because this was the will of God, for Him to be tested to show that even if He was tested by the devil himself that, in the end, He would be able to conquer all temptations. This helps us to know that if Jesus was able to be tempted in all the ways, He also knows how to defeat them all. He can help us to have victory over all temptations and He can even show us how.

In addition to this, in Acts 13:2 it is written how the Holy Spirit told them to separate Barnabas and Saul. This separation was for the separation of the work that He had to accomplish through them. When the Holy Spirit guides you to do something, this means that it is according to what God's plan is with you. If we take a look at the passage in Acts 8:29, Philip was guided to go and find a chariot on the road. He did not understand why he needed to do it, all he knew was that he must go. Because he decided to listen and follow this guidance of the Holy Spirit, he was able to spread the message of Christ to the eunuch, the eunuch listened and accepted Jesus Christ as his Lord and was baptized in water.

Philip wasn't sure why, but because he was told to go he listened, and a man gave his life to God. Because he listened and went to spread the good news, the Holy Spirit was able to further the gospel. This may happen to you as well. We need to allow ourselves to be guided by the Holy Spirit, and by doing so you might save not just one but many souls someday.

Furthermore, in Acts 20:22 it shows us that they were bound in the Spirit to go to Jerusalem, and they listened. In the passage, it says that even though they went, they did not know what will be there or what they would encounter there either. We need to realize that being guided by the Spirit does not mean you will always know what you will be doing or why you were sent. All you do know is that you must go, for the Spirit of the Lord is telling you to go. In Romans 8:14, it is written that all that are led by the Spirit of God are the Sons of God. If you want to be considered a son or daughter of the Lord God, you must allow yourself to surrender all to Him and be guided by the Holy Spirit in the direction He pleases. This will allow you to fulfill God's purpose and calling for you.

Holy Spirit the Helper

- Romans 8:26 - Likewise the Spirit also helpeth our infirmities: for we know not what we should pray for as we ought: but the Spirit itself maketh intercession for us with groanings which cannot be uttered.
- Romans 15:19 - Through mighty signs and wonders, by the power of the Spirit of God; so that from Jerusalem, and round about unto Illyricum, I have fully preached the gospel of Christ.
- Hebrew 13:6 - So that we may boldly say, The Lord is my helper, and I will not fear what man shall do unto me.
- Acts 1:8 - But ye shall receive power, after that the Holy Ghost is come upon you: and ye shall be witnesses unto me

141

both in Jerusalem, and in all Judaea, and in Samaria, and unto the uttermost part of the earth.

- Acts 2:4 - And they were all filled with the Holy Ghost, and began to speak with other tongues, as the Spirit gave them utterance.
- Acts 6:8 - And Stephen, full of faith and power, did great wonders and miracles among the people.

First, we need to distinguish 'helping' versus 'guiding.' When we defined 'being guided' it was as being led by the Spirit - all you do is follow. Yes, in a form, this is helping you, but when you are led, it means that the Spirit of the Lord is doing the work and you are following. When the Spirit of the Lord 'helps,' it means you are doing the work with Him helping. Jesus and Philip were led and they followed the Spirit in their journeys. But the Spirit helped them once they needed help, strength, or power. For example, during the time of temptation for Jesus or when Philip needed understanding of Scripture when he was speaking to the eunuch.

In Acts 6:8, it says that Stephen was filled in faith and power. This power and faith he had with the help from the Holy Spirit to do the great wonders and miracles that he did around the people. Acts 2:4 and 1:8 says that they were filled with the Spirit; this filling is power and strength (help) from the Holy Spirit to do the work needed to be done. You are going forward to do His will and the Holy Spirit is giving you the power and strength that will help you to do the will of the Father. In Hebrews 13:6, it says that the Lord is my Helper - our Lord said that if He does not go, He would not have been able to send the helper (Holy Spirit). The Lord is our Helper, through the Holy Spirit that He has put in us.

If we continue in Scripture, in Romans 15:19 Paul says that through the power of God's Spirit he was able to go and do wonders and mighty works and preach the Gospel. The Holy Spirit helps us go and expand God's Kingdom on earth, until He returns.

We should think about why we need help and why the Holy Spirit needs to help us. Help is necessary when you realize you are not able to do what needs to be done by yourself. Help can only be given to a man or woman that has decided to humble themselves, knowing they need help to achieve a goal or to do something. In Romans 8:26, it says that the helper will help us in our infirmities. This means in our weakness or sickness, what we are not able to do alone or understand by ourselves. He will help us and give us power and strength in overcoming our flaws.

Through the works we do, we are justified, meaning that we need to understand as children of God that we will need help in doing the will of God. This help includes being led by the Spirit, but also the power and strength in us given by the Spirit for us to be able to be true witnesses for Christ and spread the Word of God to all. For us to be able to crucify our flesh and to grow with Christ. The help we need to get stronger in Christ's work.

Holy Spirit the Comforter

- John 14:16 - And I will pray the Father, and he shall give you another Comforter, that he may abide with you for ever...
- John 14:26 - But the Comforter, which is the Holy Ghost, whom the Father will send in my name, he shall teach you

143

all things, and bring all things to your remembrance, whatsoever I have said unto you.

- John 15:26 - But when the Comforter is come, whom I will send unto you from the Father, even the Spirit of truth, which proceedeth from the Father, he shall testify of me...
- John 16:7 - Nevertheless I tell you the truth; It is expedient for you that I go away: for if I go not away, the Comforter will not come unto you; but if I depart, I will send him unto you.
- 2 Corinthians 1:4 - Who comforteth us in all our tribulation, that we may be able to comfort them which are in any trouble, by the comfort wherewith we ourselves are comforted of God.

The Holy Spirit will also be your comforter. I would say, out of the many things that the Holy Spirit is, this is one of the few that we understand easily as to how it applies in our lives, because when we go through many problems and situations we get comfort from our family members and friends and, even, coworkers sometimes. We understand the position of comforter fairly well.

The definition for "comforter" is someone that provides consolation or reduces the intensity of fear, anger, hatred, feeling lost, or confused in a situation or problem in life. In a way, a comforter is a reliever of the problem. In John 14:16, Jesus says, "I will pray and he will give you another comforter;" this comforter is the Holy Spirit.

As children of God, we go through much hardship and many difficulties in life. Someone that stays true to the Word of God and builds their fellowship with Christ will be some one

144

that will struggle. If you or anyone else have ever said that being a Christian is easy and you believed it, I will tell you, right now, to look at yourself for, most likely, you are not following Christ. You may ask how is this possible or how can I say this?

Someone that follows Christ is someone that must crucify their body every day. They must say 'no' to their desires, their wants and needs and put God's desires, wants, and needs first. Jesus says that you must pick up your cross and follow Him; if this is true, then you must understand that following God is not an easy task. It is very difficult for someone to say 'no' to what they want and desire in life and pick up God's will - to crucify that flesh and pick up the cross of suffering.

When you follow God, you must stay away from worldly activities, parties, and events that do not serve God or, even worse, reject God from being there. This may include birthday parties or weddings with alcohol, drugs, or with things that are inappropriate for a child of God to do. We must not take part in these. We must be willing to examine our vocabulary, our thoughts, and our actions in our daily life to follow Christ. By doing this, we may be persecuted, or hated, or gossiped about that we are 'taking life too seriously' with God.

This is why we have a comforter: for situations in our lives when it is difficult to follow God all the way to the end, even if it means death, just as we read with Stephen in the Bible. He died, but he died with joy, because no one can ask God to forgive the sins of his executioners other than people that are filled with love from God and joy in knowing who God really is. By doing this, the comforter will come, He will comfort us, He will relieve our pain or suffering, and He will make us feel empowered and welcomed in the kingdom of God.

In your life maybe you have been hated, or lost in your life, or others maybe have wanted to even kill you for following God, just as I have encountered in my life. When you stay true and unwavering in the Word of God people will see this. They will respond back with force, with anger or hateful comments and this sometimes brings us to a place of discouragement, feeling alone or depressed in that situation.

But let's give thanks to our Lord, for He has sent us a comforter to be with us in those situations and to lift us back to joy and understanding that we are children of God and we have everlasting life with Him! He will pick us out of the hole we may be in. When He does this, you will understand even more what God has done for you and you will be filled with more love for Christ and be comforted more because you are able to sacrifice some of your life for Him.

Holy Spirit the Testifier of Jesus Christ

- John 15:26 - But when the Comforter is come, whom I will send unto you from the Father, even the Spirit of truth, which proceedeth from the Father, he shall testify of me...

John 15:26 says that the comforter, which is the Holy Spirit, will also testify/witness of Jesus Christ. Someone that testifies is someone that bears witness and gives evidence for a specific cause. Just as we see in trials during a court case, there are people that testify of what has happened in a certain situation. Based off this testimony, they will either convict someone as guilty or not guilty, based on how convincing the testimony was. This is what the Holy Spirit does; He will testify

146

of Jesus Christ and who He is, what He has done, where He has gone, and where He came from.

The Holy Spirit is the Spirit of the Father, meaning the Father of Jesus. This means that the Holy Spirit, who will testify of Jesus Christ to us, is the one that has been from the beginning of times, He knows all. He will testify to us that Jesus Christ is the Son of God, that He died, that He did raise from the dead. That He is at the right hand of the Father. He will testify everything that Christ has done and by doing so we will have a true testimony of knowing who Jesus Christ is. From Titus 1:2, we know that God cannot lie - this means also that His Spirit cannot lie either, meaning when the Holy Spirit, the Testifier, comes and He testifies to you and me what Jesus Christ did, the Son of God, we can know for a fact that it is true.

It is time to allow the Holy Spirit to testify of the truth and no longer allow ourselves to be guided and lead by others. We need to realize that theology and philosophy come from the study of what man thinks, his interpretation, of what God said or meant and may not be guided by the Holy Ghost. This should cause us to always test what we are reading with the Holy Spirit. We need to start allowing the Holy Spirit to speak and testify what God has said and meant and testify of the real truth. We must stand and grow in our spiritual life and then the Holy Spirit will start speaking the truth and testifying the truth to us. This will keep us from being deceived by false teachers and others that say they know the Word of God, for we will know the Word of God as the Holy Spirit revealed it to us, not as man interprets it.

Holy Spirit the Teacher

- John 14:26 - But the Comforter, which is the Holy Ghost, whom the Father will send in my name, he shall teach you all things, and bring all things to your remembrance, whatsoever I have said unto you.
- 1 John 2:27 - But the anointing which ye have received of him abideth in you, and ye need not that any man teach you: but as the same anointing teacheth you of all things, and is truth, and is no lie, and even as it hath taught you, ye shall abide in him.

A teacher is someone that demonstrates and explains how to accomplish some type of task. The Holy Spirit will educate you on procedure or on how to put things together. He will give you the skills or discipline to understand how to do a task. Say, for example, you are studying the Word of God and you come to a specific subject, let's say the subject of "the cross." A teacher will start pointing out to you how to put together what the cross means, what it indicates, what it fulfilled. He will show you a verse and ask you what it means, as in, when you read this passage, what do you get from it? After this, He will direct you to another passage, and little by little you will put all of them together to learn the subject of the cross.

In John 14:26 it says that the Holy Spirit will teach you 'all things.' 'All things' is considered what "I have said unto you," meaning He will teach us and give us counsel unto understanding, to have wisdom of God and how to understand the cross, what Jesus Christ did, why He did it, and much more. A teacher is one that has wisdom and knowledge and gives wisdom to us to put things together. He will teach us how to read the Scripture, how to put concepts together. He will clarify what is murky to us or what is in the dark and hidden that we do not understand. If we don't understand the Trinity, the cross, love, fruits, sanctification, justification, creation or any other topic, the Holy Spirit is the one that will help us decipher those, just like a puzzle, until it is finished for us to understand what we are looking at.

We need to stand as children of God and allow the Spirit of the Lord to start teaching us what is true, what is right, what is pure in front of God and become wise and knowledgeable; able to understand ideas based on what the Holy Spirit has taught us through the Scripture rather than what man can teach us – ideas which come from the mind of man and may be false if they are not led by the Spirit of the Lord.

Holy Spirit the Instructor

- Nehemiah 9:19-20 -Yet thou in thy manifold mercies forsookest them not in the wilderness: the pillar of the cloud departed not from them by day, to lead them in the way; neither the pillar of fire by night, to shew them light, and the way wherein they should go. Thou gavest also thy good spirit to instruct them, and withheldest not thy manna from their mouth, and gavest them water for their thirst.
- Acts 8:29 - Then the Spirit said unto Philip, Go near, and join thyself to this chariot.

I would like to clarify, first, the difference between a teacher and an instructor - many people will assume they are the same, but they are not. A teacher will educate you on *how* to do something, while an instructor is more like a coach, he will *tell* you what to do. Think about it this way: when a teacher educates you, you will understand what you are doing, while an instructor will tell you just what to do and you might not even understand what you are doing.

An example of the Holy Spirit as an instructor is in Acts 8:29, when the Holy Spirit instructed Philip to go and join himself to this chariot. The Holy Spirit instructed him, and he listened even though he did not understand what he was doing. Just like a coach does at practice; he will tell you to do something even when you do not understand what you are getting out of it by listening or what it will benefit you with, but because he instructs you, you will listen.

In Nehemiah 9, it says that He instructed the Israelites with His Spirit, to do what? To follow the pillar of fire by night and the pillar of cloud by day. He told them what to do.

Now, in the process of being instructed you can also be taught. After Philip join himself to the chariot in Acts, he realized what he must do and spoke to the eunuch. As children of God, we are familiar with this concept because there are times when we are called by the Holy Spirit to go somewhere and even we do not know why we are going, but because we are instructed to go by God we listen and go. Once we are there, we realize because we listened we had a chance to help someone, or even change a person's life when they accept Jesus Christ as a personal savior, just as the eunuch did in the passage from Acts. Philip was instructed, he listened, and because he did, a man learned about the Son of God and was saved and baptized. We need to do what we are instructed by God to do even when we may not understand it to the fullest. By doing so, we will do God's will, and some, including yourself, may be blessed.

If we stand firm in listening to the instruction of the Holy Spirit in our life, we will be led to the truth and into the will of the Father. We will make a change in the kingdom of God, and the kingdom of the devil will start falling apart. If we do what we are instructed, others will see that God is manifesting Himself among His children and real transformation will take place.

Holy Spirit the Speaker

- Matthew 10:19-20 -But when they deliver you up, take no thought how or what ye shall speak: for it shall be given you in that same hour what ye shall speak. For it is not ye that speak, but the Spirit of your Father which speaketh in you.
- Revelation 2:7 - He that hath an ear, let him hear what the Spirit saith unto the churches; To him that overcometh will I give to eat of the tree of life, which is in the midst of the paradise of God.
- Acts 8:19 - Then the Spirit said unto Philip, Go near, and join thyself to this chariot.

Here are only a few verses that show the Holy Spirit speaking through us or to us. In Acts 8, it says that the Spirit said to Philip to get up and join himself to the chariot. There are times in our life when the Spirit of the Lord speaks to us, reveals things to us, tells us what to do, or gives us an understanding of what to do. We are able to fulfill God's will in delivering someone, to encourage someone, or even encourage ourselves in certain situations, just as Philip and others did when they heard a clear voice speaking to them. The problem is, many times, that we ourselves are not spiritually aware in hearing the voice of God for we have not allowed ourselves to grow and wait on the Spirit to speak.

In Matthew 10, we see that the Holy Spirit is also the one that can speak through us in situations for people to receive God's message for them. As a preacher and teacher, there are many times when I know the Holy Spirit has taken over and speaks through me to others to fulfill His plan and for them to get the answers they are looking for. In Matthew 10, it says do not worry what you should speak in certain situations, for it will be given to you by the Spirit of the Father; meaning there are times that you may not know what to say, but because the Holy Spirit lives in you, He will give you the words that will need to be said in that situation. This only can happen once you exercise your spiritual awareness to the voice of God.

Once you and I start allowing the Holy Spirit to speak through us, this will manifest the power of the living God, and others will see that when God speaks, it is the truth and people will not be able to deny it. When the Holy Spirit will speak, people will be convicted of their sins, transgressions, and iniquities against the true God and they will believe, be saved, and be baptized in His name, and the Kingdom of God will grow.

Holy Spirit the Revealer

- 1 Corinthians 2:9-10 – But as it is written, Eye hath not seen, nor ear heard, neither have entered into the heart of man, the things which God hath prepared for them that love him. But God hath revealed them unto us by his Spirit: for the Spirit searcheth all things, yea, the deep things of God.

- John 14:25-26 - These things have I spoken unto you, being yet present with you. But the Comforter, which is the Holy Ghost, whom the Father will send in my name, he shall teach you all things, and bring all things to your remembrance, whatsoever I have said unto you.
- Revelation- The entire book of Revelation was revealed through the Holy Spirit to John.

The Holy Spirit is a revealer of truth and of God's will, or plan, for what has to happen for the world and for each one of us personally in the present and future and even what has happened in the past. A revealer is someone that makes something be known, discloses, or divulges what is happening. In 1 Corinthians 2, we see that through the Spirit of God that He may reveal to us what He has prepared for us and others, for the ones that love Him. In John 14, we see that when the Holy Spirit comes, it will teach what is true and of God; that in itself is a revelation of what is true.

One of the most impactful books in the Bible is the book of Revelation. The book is a compilation of the visions John had of what will come to pass, including the end times. We see in Scripture that the Spirit of the Lord works in vision and dreams with other forms as well; these forms give the children of God insight into what God has planned or what might come to pass. These are revelations given to us to know what may come to pass in the next moments or days, for the children of God to prepare.

Just as it did for Peter in Acts 10:19: he had a vision that told him three men were coming and that he must go with them. In Acts 18:9, Paul had a vision of encouragement from the Lord.

Another example would be in Acts 9:10-12, where Ananias had a vision to go and meet Saul to heal him, and at the same time Saul had a vision as well that Ananias was coming to him. Visions and dreams can be given to fulfill God's purpose and to reveal to us things we need to be ready for.

When we allow ourselves to be open to the work of the Holy Spirit through the revealer, we will allow ourselves to be prepared for God's work even more. Being prepared means that we will be equipped even further to do the will of the Father but also be fully equipped to go against the kingdom of the devil. And when the Holy Spirit reveals things to us, we will know the truth of God.

Holy Spirit the Filler

- Acts 4:31 - And when they had prayed, the place was shaken where they were assembled together; and they were all filled with the Holy Ghost, and they spake the word of God with boldness.
- Ephesians 5:18-21 - And be not drunk with wine, wherein is excess; but be filled with the Spirit; Speaking to yourselves in psalms and hymns and spiritual songs, singing and making melody in your heart to the Lord; Giving thanks always for all things unto God and the Father in the name of our Lord Jesus Christ; Submitting yourselves one to another in the fear of God.

The Holy Spirit is the one that fills us when we are empty. Being empty of the Holy Spirit means that someone was not filled with joyfulness from the Lord. In Acts 4, it says when they were filled, they were able to speak with boldness. Meaning that when you are filled with the Spirit you will have so much

154

joy in your heart for the Lord that you will be able to speak God's word with boldness, for this joy is overpowering in your life.

When we look at Ephesians 5:18-21, we see that it says not to be drunk with wine for this does not produce goodness. Instead, it tells us to be filled with the Spirit and it says being filled will bring speaking in Psalms, singing of hymns, and spiritual songs - for you are joyful with the Spirit. It continues, saying to make melody in your heart to the Lord. Furthermore, the passage says to give thanks always for all things and submit yourself to God in fear (the word fear here means awe/reverence of God).

Once you are filled with the Spirit, it brings on a true happiness and joyfulness because of who God is in your life and it will make you want to praise and worship God with everything and give thanks for what He has done. This joy and happiness will bring a spark, a light, into your life that others will see in you and cause them to ponder on why you are so joyful in God and make them want what you have.

Allow yourself to be filled, stay in God's presence. For when you are in His presence, that is when you will truly be happy. That is when you will be able to shine brighter and bring forth good fruits for the Lord, your God. This is what allows all to see that you truly believe and love your God.

Holy Spirit the Interceder/Advocate

- John15:26 - But when the Comforter/Advocate/interceder is come, whom I will send unto you from the Father, even the Spirit of truth, which proceedeth from the Father, he shall testify of me...

155

- Romans 8:26 - Likewise the Spirit also helpeth our infirmities: for we know not what we should pray for as we ought: but the Spirit itself maketh intercession for us with groanings which cannot be uttered.

In our life, the Holy Spirit acts as our advocate/interceder on our behalf. An interceder/advocate is someone that comes on or behalf and does something on our behalf, he does what we can't. Here, the word in Greek for comforter is 'par-ak'-lay-tos,' this word means advocate, interceder, as well as comforter and helper. For the purpose of understanding the Holy Spirit's function here, we need to understand what each one of these means. He helps us in our infirmities, weakness, and our sicknesses. When you and I are too weak or are unable to, or do not even know how to, do something the Holy Spirit comes on our behalf and He intercedes. He comes to do what we are not able to do. If we are not able to pray and we don't know what to say or even how to say it, the Holy Spirit comes and He prays for you and me, for our Father in Heaven to hear us.

If you and I have sinned, and we are in much pain and suffering from it, the Holy Spirit is the one that will also pray with you for forgiveness and give you the words to say or He will pray for you, on your behalf, to the Father.

Imagine! The Spirit of the Lord our God is praying for us when we are too weak or are not able to pray for ourselves. He goes in front of the Father for us in groanings which cannot be uttered and that we do not know.

Do not be afraid when you are no longer able to speak the words that must come out, or do not have words any longer

156

to pray. Instead, start praying for the Holy Spirit to intercede for you and give you words for what you need to do. To give glory, worship, praise, honor, thanksgiving, and repentance of sin. The Spirit is willing to come and be your interceder.

Holy Spirit the Caller

- Acts 13:2 - As they ministered to the Lord, and fasted, the Holy Ghost said, Separate me Barnabas and Saul for the work whereunto I have called them.
- John 3:8 - The wind bloweth where it listeth, and thou hearest the sound thereof, but canst not tell whence it cometh, and whither it goeth: so is every one that is born of the Spirit.

We may not understand that the Holy Spirit also calls us. The Holy Spirit calls, cries to us for the will of the Father to be done. In Acts 13, we see that it says that the Holy Ghost told them to separate Barnabas and Saul for the work which He has called them to do. There are times when we know the Holy Spirit is telling us our calling and that we must go do it, but we deny it. Even so, He keeps on calling, He keeps on crying out to us to continue in the work for which He has called us.

When we read John 3, we see that it compares the Holy Spirit to wind: it says you hear it but do not know where it comes from or where it goes and it says that is the same for all those that are born of the Spirit. This verse is saying that when you are led by the Spirit of God you can hear it and feel it, but you don't know how it comes. Earlier, we spoke about Philip, how the Spirit instructed him to go and join himself to the chariot, and that he was going without knowing why. If you are led by the Spirit there will be a time that will come that you will feel a pulling, a nudge, to go somewhere: this is the calling, the urging of the Spirit to do the will of God.

We need to listen when we hear the calling for when we do, we are in the will of God; when we don't, we are no longer in the will of God, and if we continue ignoring the Holy Spirit's call, we may become numb to what God has called us to do. When we become numb, we may never feel it or hear the calling again. If this happens, then we may never come back to what He has called us to do in His kingdom. This leads us to damaging the kingdom of God rather than building it up.

Holy Spirit the Strengthener by Might

- Ephesians 3:16 – That he would grant you, according to the riches of his glory, to be strengthened with might by his Spirit in the inner man.
- Acts 1:8 - But ye shall receive power, after that the Holy Ghost is come upon you: and ye shall be witnesses unto me both in Jerusalem, and in all Judaea, and in Samaria, and unto the uttermost part of the earth.

There are a few that considerer strength and might as two different things. On my part, I am combining them together for they are intertwined with each other. On the path of following our Lord, we will encounter battles against the enemy, whether this comes from men or Lucifer himself. Because of this, the Holy Spirit will strengthen us, through His might (power). In Ephesians 3, it says that the inner man will be strengthened by the Spirit, which is the Spirit of the Lord. This is what keeps us going, it is what makes us keep pushing forward through the enemy and the strongholds of the devil. Our strength to go forward is built through the power of the Holy Spirit that He releases to us.

In Acts, it says that when the Holy Ghost will come upon you that you will receive power (might). And it says that this power will help us be witnesses unto both Jerusalem and all the way to the end of the world. In doing the work of God, there are times where we encounter times of hardship, times of difficulties and, no matter what it seems like we do, we are blocked. Now, many times, the problem with this is that we ourselves are trying to go forward with our strength and not the power that God has given us. This power/might that the Holy Spirit releases down on us, gives us the strength, the courage to keep moving forward in the Kingdom of God.

We need to allow ourselves to no longer be controlled by our strength and what we can do, for we are dead without Christ and if it wasn't for Him allowing us to breathe another breath, we would not be here. If we stop depending on our strength and power and allow ourselves to be filled with the power of the Holy Ghost, we will be empowered and strengthened to do God's will. And we will be able to move mountains, for it is God working in His unlimited power, in His Spirit, and not man.

Holy Spirit brings Joy

- 1 Thessalonians 1:6 - And ye became followers of us, and of the Lord, having received the word in much affliction, with joy of the Holy Ghost.
- Hebrews 1:9 – Thou hast loved righteousness, and hated iniquity; therefore God, even thy God, hath anointed thee with the oil of gladness above thy fellows.

159

- Acts 13:52 - And the disciples were filled with joy, and with the Holy Ghost.
- Acts 16:25 - And at midnight Paul and Silas prayed, and sang praises unto God: and the prisoners heard them.

When we have the Holy Spirit, it brings a joy to our lives that we cannot explain or describe. In 1 Thessalonians, we see that it says that they received the word with much affliction and pain but, even so, they were filled with joy from the Holy Ghost. When you and I have the beautiful Holy Spirit that lives in us, it brings a joy that cannot be explained; even through pain and suffering, even through beatings, as we see in Scripture that they received, and yet we can have joy.

In Hebrews 1, it says that they were anointed with Oil (Holy Spirit) of Gladness. The same in Acts 13:52 - the disciples were filled with joy and the Holy Spirit indicated that they had joy for the Holy Spirit was with them. In Acts 16, it says that Paul and Silas (in prison) were praying and singing praises to God. How? Because they had joy in them from the Holy Spirit. Even in circumstances of imprisonment from doing the work of God, they were still filled with joy and gave glory to God.

There are times that people see us with joy even through the hardship and difficulties. This is because we have the living God living in us, through the Holy Spirit, that brings life, joy, love, and peace into our lives no matter what is happening.

If the children of God came together in joy no matter what situation we were in, and realized that even in death that the person which has God living in him is still alive and in a better place than you and I, if when we were in sickness or in situations that usually bring depression or tears, we were able to replace that with the joy from the Spirit of God that lives in us, then we would have joy no matter what comes along. Many will turn to God for they will see that in life where people are usually in tears and in pain or suffering, that God's children are joyful for God is with them no matter what and He does not forsake His children.

Holy Spirit the Bringer of Freedom

- 2 Corinthians 3:17 – Now the Lord is that Spirit: and where the Spirit of the Lord is, there is liberty.
- John 8:36 - If the Son therefore shall make you free, ye shall be free indeed.
- Romans 8:10 - And if Christ be in you, the body is dead because of sin; but the Spirit is life because of righteousness.
- 1 John 4:4 - Ye are of God, little children, and have overcome them: because greater is he that is in you, than he that is in the world.

The Spirit of the Lord brings freedom and liberty to all that want to accept Him. John speaks that if Christ sets anyone free, He will be free indeed. If you have been set free, whatever bondage or chain or possession that was pulling you down and dragging you around, not allowing you to have the life that was given to you, that bondage has been broken; that means you have been set free and are able to give full glory to God. We have been set free from sin and death and we have been brought to righteousness, into life. In 1 John, it says that greater is He that is in you, which is the Holy Spirit living in us and through us, than that of this world and the devil.

We need to realize that if you and I are children of God that means that what He has given us, the Holy Spirit, is greater than anything else that is out there. Greater than addiction, greater than the flesh's desire, greater than the world, greater than the devil, greater than demons. For what is in you and I is greater and more powerful than any of these and we are able to conquer with the help of the Holy Spirit.

If the children of God step up and understand what happened on the cross and with the resurrection, we would be living in a completely different atmosphere. We would understand what was achieved and accomplished and we would be filled with a true freedom and understand that, if you are in addiction, that God has given you a greater power in you that is able to conquer it. If you live in consistent sin, God has given you a greater power that lives in you to break free, and be free indeed, from it.

When God sets you truly free, you are free, but if you do not replace what bondage was broken, whatever you have been set free from can come back if you allow yourself to fall back into it. Just as if you have been set free from jail, the bondage you have been in, if you allow yourself, you can end up back in the same bondage which you were set free from before.

We need to realize that if God has set you free, it is time to step up and fill up that area of your life with better friends, church, the Word of God, prayer, fasting, and worship in front of God so as to keep your freedom, to never fall back again or allow the devil to deceive you in any way or form. Fill your soul and spirit with life and you will be desiring the Kingdom of God rather than the devil's. For what is in you and I is greater than any force out there; once we understand this, we will be able to be fully free from any bondage and chain, anything that has been holding you back.

Holy Spirit Helps us to Obey

- 1 Peter 1:22 - Seeing ye have purified your souls in obeying the truth through the Spirit unto unfeigned love of the brethren, see that ye love one another with a pure heart fervently...
- Romans 8:12-14 - Therefore, brethren, we are debtors, not to the flesh, to live after the flesh. For if ye live after the flesh, ye shall die: but if ye through the Spirit do mortify the deeds of the body, ye shall live. For as many as are led by the Spirit of God, they are the sons of God.
- Galatian 5:16 - This I say then, Walk in the Spirit, and ye shall not fulfil the lust of the flesh.
- Ezekiel 36:27 - And I will put my spirit within you, and cause you to walk in my statutes, and ye shall keep my judgments, and do them.

The word 'obey' is a word used when someone decides to listen and do what someone tells them to do. It is submitting yourself to authority and accepting what you must do. In 1 Peter 1, it says that we can purify our soul by obeying the truth, which is done through the Spirit. The Spirit of the Lord helps us obey the Word of the Lord. If we look in Ezekiel 36:27, God says He will put His Spirit within them and this will cause (reason, motive, conviction) them to follow His statutes. This doesn't mean He will force you to do His will or to follow Him, but it means it will give us a motive, a reason, it will make you and I feel God's presence and understand His statues. The Spirit will give conviction for us to realize what is wrong - we will feel it, we will know, but it is still up to us to obey.

Romans 8 shows us that we kill sin by the Spirit. This means that the Spirit will help us to kill the sin by obeying what the Spirit tells us and what we feel through Him. A person that feels guilt will feel bad and sorry for what they have done or what may happen, and this guilt will cause us to make the right choice in front of God, and by the Spirit we will obey.

If we look into Galatians 5:16, it says walk in the Spirit and you will not do the lust of the flesh. The word 'IN' is translated wrong, it should be 'BY.' Meaning we walk *by* the Spirit, which is different. *By* the Spirit we will obey and not do the lust of the flesh. If we allow the Spirit of the Lord to take over, we will start obeying what the Lord has told us to do; we will obey God's commands rather than disobeying what He has told us to do.

By obeying what God has said to do, others will see that we are not hypocrites and that we follow what God has said, that we are not two-faced, but what we say we also do and live by the Word of God. By doing this, others will see that a true child of God listens and obeys themselves, rather than spending their time judging others for whatever they might be doing.

Holy Spirit Lives in Us (Eternal Life)

- 1 Corinthians 3:16 - Know ye not that ye are the temple of God, and that the Spirit of God dwelleth in you?

- 1 Corinthians 6:19 - What? know ye not that your body is the temple of the Holy Ghost which is in you, which ye have of God, and ye are not your own?
- 2 Timothy 1:14 - That good thing which was committed unto thee keep by the Holy Ghost which dwelleth in us.
- Romans 8:9-11 - But ye are not in the flesh, but in the Spirit, if so be that the Spirit of God dwell in you. Now if any man have not the Spirit of Christ, he is none of his. And if Christ be in you, the body is dead because of sin; but the Spirit is life because of righteousness. But if the Spirit of him that raised up Jesus from the dead dwell in you, he that raised up Christ from the dead shall also quicken your mortal bodies by his Spirit that dwelleth in you.

The Spirit of the Lord lives/dwells in you and me. Just as we dwell in a home and that is where we live, where we clean, where we eat, and build a relationship with our family. In 1 Corinthians 3, it is written that our bodies are the temple of God and that His Spirit dwells in us. This means that our Lord, the Creator of all, the King of kings, and the Alpha and Omega lives in us and that is where He stays, to eat, clean, and build a relationship with His children.

In 2 Timothy 1, the passage says to keep the good things which were committed to us, and to keep it by the Holy Spirit that dwells in us. To keep the good work of salvation and His true and sound words that were given by God and keep it by the Holy Spirit.

When we continue and read Romans 8:9-11, we see that we live in the Spirit, for the Spirit of the Lord is in us. It goes on, saying that if we do not have the Spirit of Christ, we do not belong to Him, we are not His children nor part of Him. But because we have the Spirit of Christ, the body is dead because of sin, but the Spirit brings us to life because of righteousness. And because this Spirit raised Jesus up, it will also raise us up because it dwells in us.

First Corinthians 6:19 states that if we are the temple of God that our body is no longer ours, but it is God's. If this body is God's we must bring it to Him as a living sacrifice, a body that is without blemish, without sin, without marks; it must be a perfect sacrifice to our Father in Heaven. We must realize that God is holy, and we must also be holy. If God is holy, we must then also live holy, for how can you expect a holy God to live in you, the One that cannot look upon sin, to dwell in you, if you're not holy?

We must clean our lives; we must consecrate ourselves and become holy so that our Holy God can live in us. If we do this, we will start seeing God's manifestation and power in our lives, for He will dwell in us. We will see Him use us in His will more and more, and the Kingdom of God will start growing through the manifestation of God's power through us.

Holy Spirit the Renewal

- Titus 3:4-7 -But after that the kindness and love of God our Saviour toward man appeared, Not by works of righteousness which we have done, but according to his mercy he saved us, by the washing of regeneration, and renewing of the Holy Ghost; Which he shed on us abundantly through Jesus Christ our Saviour; That being justified by his grace, we should be made heirs according to the hope of eternal life.

166

- Ephesians 4:23 - And be renewed in the spirit of your mind...
- Romans 12:2 - And be not conformed to this world: but be ye transformed by the renewing of your mind, that ye may prove what is that good, and acceptable, and perfect, will of God.
- 2 Corinthians 4:16 - For which cause we faint not; but though our outward man perish, yet the inward man is renewed day by day.

The Holy Spirit brings into our lives a renewing, a regeneration. Being regenerated is the process of making anew what has been slowly decaying. Think about a plant in a garden: the more time that goes by without it being fed its fertilizer or watered to keep it maintained, the more it shrivels up, it starts to bend over and can even start decaying. When you start giving it water and feeding the plant it starts to come back to life, it starts to regenerate and become renewed back to its fruitful, producing state. This is what the Holy Spirit does in us.

Ephesians 4 tell us to be renewed in the Spirit of our mind. We must allow the Spirit to renew our minds of heaviness, of doubt, or of confusion – to be restored from a state of decaying back to the state of regenerating, to come back to a proper state. In Romans 12, it tells us not to transform to the world but be transformed by the renewing of our minds which will allow us to be proof of what is acceptable and perfect in the will of God.

When we look in 2 Corinthians 4:16, it is an encouraging verse, saying that even though the outward man will perish, the inner man, which is our soul and Spirit, will be renewed day by day. What a great verse! No matter what, when we allow the Spirit of the Lord to take over, He will renew our soul and spirit to a state of being acceptable for the perfect will of God. It will come to a state of truly depending on God, a state of relying on the Father, a state of desiring to do the will of the Father, a state of joy and gladness that you are a child of God and have everlasting life that He has given through His mercy, grace, and love.

When we allow the Holy Spirit to renew us, to regenerate us, in our mind and soul, we will have a clear picture of the will of God. We will be led to the desire of the will of God in our lives. We will truly want to live the will of God, the road that He has put in front of you to follow, a road that was laid down before you were even born. This renewing will bring a willing, full soul to obeying the Father, a joy of understanding that His will and His path, that He chosen for you, is the best plan and you will make yourself follow it no matter what.

Holy Spirit the Producer of Fruits

- Galatians 5:22-23 - But the fruit of the Spirit is love, joy, peace, longsuffering, gentleness, goodness, faith, Meekness, temperance: against such there is no law.

The Holy Spirit produces fruits in us. These fruits can be taken as a product and character of people that allow themselves to bring forth fruits. The fruits of the Spirit are what many people desire to have in their life. This is because the fruits in our daily life would bring such a comfort to us and encourage a life of unfailing faith in the work of God.

If the children of God allowed the Spirit, which dwells in us, to start manifesting the Fruit of Love towards all, the Fruit of Joy in our daily life, and the Fruit of Peace in our lives, we would already be living a life that our Lord is shining through and visible.

If we lived a life also producing the Fruit of Longsuffering, Gentleness, and Goodness in our lives, our God would be seen even more. When we go even further and live in the Fruit of true Faith, Meekness, and Temperance, our God will be shining so bright and we, His children, will have such a strong and pleasant aroma that others around us will want to accept Jesus Christ as their Lord, to live like we do.

In our generation, I would say that most of the nine fruits mentioned here are not seen in the children of God and because of this many turn away from following God. I knew someone that was invited to a church service and, instead of coming, they responded with a letter saying that if the church acts like the world does and doesn't produce the fruits of the Spirit then why should they give their life to Christ, when even the congregation doesn't produce what it should and doesn't live set apart? They never came, for the church was not behaving according to the Word of God.

We need to step down and allow the Holy Spirit to be in control, to start producing what should be produced from a child of God. If we start doing this, I believe many will see it and turn and follow God with their whole hearts for they will see a difference in the children of God.

Holy Spirit the One who Convicts

- John 16:8-11 - and when he is come, he will reprove the world of sin, and of righteousness, and of judgment: Of sin, because they believe not on me; Of righteousness, because I go to my Father, and ye see me no more; Of judgment, because the prince of this world is judged.

- Hebrews 4:12 - For the word of God is quick, and powerful, and sharper than any two-edged sword, piercing even to the dividing asunder of soul and spirit, and of the joints and marrow, and is a discerner of the thoughts and intents of the heart.

This is one of the most known or common views that many Christians have today about the Holy Spirit; that when He comes, He will come and convict the world. To convict someone is to know that what they have been doing in their life is wrong and to call them out on it. Beforehand, someone might have believed something they were doing was wrong, but when they are confronted with the truth, with the Word of God, they are convicted and realize, without a doubt, that what they have been doing is sinful in front of God and they must change.

In John 16, the passage refers to the Holy Spirit coming to convict the world of sin. When He comes, you will understand what sin is and what is of righteousness and judgment. The Holy Spirit will not only convict you of your sin and what you do wrongfully but He will also convict you of what is not righteous and what you have done until that moment, believing it was right, and will show you the judgement that lies ahead if you continue on that path. There are many that believe what they are doing is right, but when He convicts you with righteousness there will be a light showing you that what you might have thought was true and right, is actually the opposite. This conviction will also bring us to the knowledge of knowing that Jesus Christ is the son of God.

In Hebrews 4:12, we read that the Word of God is powerful and quick and sharper than any two-edged sword and when it is spoken, when the Holy Spirit convicts you, when you hear the Word of God, it will cut your soul and spirit. You will be able to discern and know the thoughts and intents of the heart and know what is wrong. The conviction we get will be a true conviction, a conviction that will lead us to the truth. If we deny what we know then, for we have heard the Word of God, we will be departing from God willingly because we want to follow our own desires.

When we are convicted of the truth and we know what is wrong, we must obey and change our lives for if we do not, we ourselves will have decided to leave God, just as it says in Hebrews 3:12. We must realize that when the Holy Spirit convicts us, it's because we are not living according to how God has commanded us to live, and He is speaking, He is telling us that we must change. If we decide to listen, if we take heed to what we have felt, we will become more holy in front of God and more acceptable to His perfect will. This will allow us to become true bearers of the light and the salt that we have been called to be.

Holy Spirit the Sanctifier

- 2 Thessalonians 2:13 - But we are bound to give thanks always to God for you, brethren beloved of the Lord, because God hath from the beginning chosen you to salvation through sanctification of the Spirit and belief of the truth...
- Romans 15:16 - That I should be the minister of Jesus Christ to the Gentiles, ministering the gospel of God, that the

171

offering up of the Gentiles might be acceptable, being sanctified by the Holy Ghost.

- 2 Corinthians 3:18 - But we all, with open face beholding as in a glass the glory of the Lord, are changed into the same image from glory to glory, even as by the Spirit of the Lord.

The Holy Spirit is the one that "sanctifies" us. This is a word that many people do not understand. To be sanctified is the action or the ability of making someone holy. This is a very important duty for the Holy Spirit in our life, just as it says in 2 Corinthians 3 that we go from glory to glory, to becoming more like Christ by the Spirit. This means that little by little we are cleansed, the Holy Spirit removes filth, dirt, uncleanness, sin, transgression, and other things out of our lives and we become more pure, holy, and sanctified in front of God.

In 2 Thessalonians 2, we see that our God from the beginning had chosen us into salvation through sanctification (holiness) by the Spirit into the Truth. This means that God has chosen you and I for everlasting life with holiness by His Spirit, for His Spirit is what makes us become more holy in front Him. Sanctification is what makes us receive favor in front of God. This happens only when His children allow themselves to be clean, and kept clean, and they look to become more holy every day. This means that we are seeking God's face, we are looking for a true relationship with our Lord. By allowing ourselves to go from glory to glory we become more holy in front of God, for we are sanctifying ourselves and the Lord our God allows His favor upon us. He listens and responds more to our prayers, for His children are looking for more, seeking Him more, to have a true relationship.

There is a warning that I need to give here: without being made holy/sanctified by the Holy Spirit you will not enter the kingdom of God. In Scripture, there are many passages that speak about what type of people will never enter the kingdom of God and this is because they are not allowing themselves to be sanctified and instead living according to their desires. In Matthew 7:21-23, it speaks about men of God that did many wonderful works, prophesied in His name and cast out demons in His name, but on the day of judgement, the Lord says to them, "I never knew you; depart from me, ye that work iniquity."

In addition, it speaks in Revelation that when you are neither hot nor cold but lukewarm, the Lord will vomit you out of His mouth. We need to realize that when we do not allow ourselves to become sanctified by the Holy Spirit, we are departing from God, and one day we will pay for that.

Holy Spirit the One Uniting

- Ephesians 4:3-4 - Endeavoring to keep the unity of the Spirit in the bond of peace. There is one body, and one Spirit, even as ye are called in one hope of your calling...
- 1 Corinthians 12:13 - For by one Spirit are we all baptized into one body, whether we be Jews or Gentiles, whether we be bond or free; and have been all made to drink into one Spirit.
- Galatians 3:26-29 - For ye are all the children of God by faith in Christ Jesus. For as many of you as have been baptized into Christ have put on Christ. There is neither Jew nor Greek, there is neither bond nor free, there is neither male nor female: for ye are all one in Christ Jesus.

- Romans 8:14-16 - For as many as are led by the Spirit of God, they are the sons of God. For ye have not received the spirit of bondage again to fear; but ye have received the Spirit of adoption, whereby we cry, Abba, Father. The Spirit itself beareth witness with our spirit, that we are the children of God...

The Spirit of the Lord is what brings us together, it is what unites us in one Spirit. When we look at the passage of Ephesians, it says that He unites us in the bond of peace, for we are one body and one Spirit. This Spirit unites us to become one no matter what color or race we are or from what kind of background we come - the Holy Spirit will unite us. When we will be together, we will know that we are brother and sister in Christ, for our Spirits are united to each other.

The passage in Romans 8 tells us that we that are led by and have the Spirit of the Lord in us, that we are daughters and sons of God. For we have received the Spirit of Adoption whereby we cry Abba (Father). Meaning that the Holy Spirit unites us, that we all have the Spirit of God by which we can call God our Father and His children are our brothers and sisters in Christ. This demonstrates a significant difference between children of God and this world. When, and if, we call ourselves children of God and we have His Spirit we must also be united with others in Christ.

This is one area, I would say, that we struggle with many times. This is the reason why there are so many different denominations and organizations out there, because the children of God are not able to unite in Spirit. The question comes, if we all have the same Spirit, why can we not join together and be united?

This is because the Spirit of God desires what the Father desires and when a group decides to follow their own views rather than God's view, this destroys the unity and splits His children from one another. It is time that we come together and understand that we all worship and come to the same God, and it is time for us to unite and show that God's kingdom is strong and united in God's Spirit. That we desire what God desires and not to fulfill man's desire. If we are able to do this, the churches of God will start uniting with one another in love, joy, and peace.

Holy Spirit the Sealer

- Ephesians 1:13-14 - In whom ye also trusted, after that ye heard the word of truth, the gospel of your salvation: in whom also after that ye believed, ye were sealed with that holy Spirit of promise, Which is the earnest of our inheritance until the redemption of the purchased possession, unto the praise of his glory.
- Romans 8:16 - The Spirit itself beareth witness with our spirit, that we are the children of God...
- John 3:16 - For God so loved the world, that he gave his only begotten Son, that whosoever believeth in him should not perish, but have everlasting life.
- 2 Corinthians 1:21-22 - Now he which stablisheth us with you in Christ, and hath anointed us, is God; Who hath also sealed us, and given the earnest of the Spirit in our hearts.

When we give our lives and ask the Lord Jesus to come into our hearts, He sends the Holy Spirit to seal us. The word 'seal' is used to define something that brings two things together and prevents them from comping apart or prevents anything from coming in between them. It secures two things together. You are sealed in the Holy Spirit once you have heard the word of truth, which is the Gospel, and afterwards have believed and accepted Christ. This seal is the promise and access of the inheritance of the redemption you have received in Jesus Christ towards the possession He will give of everlasting life.

In the passage of Romans 8, it tells us that the Spirit itself is what bears witness, with our spirit, that we are the children of God. This shows us that once we have the Spirit in us, it will be our advocate that we are the children of God, that we are His, that we have the promise, the inheritance in Jesus Christ. Just as in John 3 it says that after we have received it, we should not perish but have everlasting life in Christ.

I would like us to realize something here: a seal can be broken. The Word of God tells us that He will never forsake us. This does not mean that you cannot forsake Him. Just as you are the one that allows Jesus to come into your life, to make this seal unto you as His child and for Him to put the Holy Spirit in you. In John 3:16 it says that we "should not perish," indicating that we will not perish if we truly believe. When you truly believe, there is always an action, an act, from you that follows, showing that you believe. This is why the Word says that you are saved by faith but justified by works.

Hebrews 3:12 tells us to heed and not have an evil heart of unbelief to depart from the living God. The only way to depart is if you were with Him in the first place. An evil heart is simply one that does not want to follow God's will, commands, statues, or His judgement. Once we do not follow what He has told us to

176

follow, we will start departing from Him, allowing ourselves to break our seal, if we continue on the path of unrighteousness, and we can lose our salvation, just as it shows in Matthew 7:21-23.

Holy Spirit the Giver of Access to the Father

- Ephesians 2:14-19 - For he is our peace, who hath made both one, and hath broken down the middle wall of partition between us; Having abolished in his flesh the enmity, even the law of commandments contained in ordinances; for to make in himself of twain one new man, so making peace; And that he might reconcile both unto God in one body by the cross, having slain the enmity thereby: And came and preached peace to you which were afar off, and to them that were nigh. For through him we both have access by one Spirit unto the Father. Now therefore ye are no more strangers and foreigners, but fellow citizens with the saints, and of the household of God...
- 2 Corinthian 5:18 - And all things are of God, who hath reconciled us to himself by Jesus Christ, and hath given to us the ministry of reconciliation...

Through the gift of the Holy Spirit we receive access to our Father in heaven. This access is the ability to enter or approach the Father and speak with Him directly. This access was also given because in 2 Corinthians 5, it says that God the Father has reconciled, or made peace, with us through Jesus Christ and, because of this, has also given us this ministry of peace. Because He made peace and sent His only begotten son to die for you and me, at the point that we believe and accept Him into our lives, the Holy Spirit starts working and gives us access to the Father.

Ephesians 2 speaks about the now broken wall of partition, which divided us from each other. When we read the Old Testament, we see that the way they communicated with God was through the High Priest, and the priests were the ones that made sacrifices, and spoke to God on the behalf of the people. Now, He has removed that barrier which did not allow us to have access directly to the Father. By sending His son to the cross, He slain the enmity which was the hostility, aggression, and unfriendliness. This was done through Him, and we have access to the Father by the Spirit of the Lord.

The Lord God has put into us a Spirit, and this Spirit has broken down the veil, the wall, and the barrier between Him and us, and has given us access to Him. We now are able to speak to the Father directly; we no longer need to go to a priest. We have access to ask for forgiveness for what we have done, we have access to speak to Him directly, and for Him to speak back to us.

We need to realize that we do have access to our Father in Heaven, but if we do not allow ourselves to be sanctified and cleansed of sin and become holy and acceptable to Him, our Father in Heaven may not speak to us. This is also why He has allowed men and women of God to have the Gifts of the Holy Spirit: to reveal more to us through prophecy, wisdom, dreams, and visions. So that we may go to those that have these gifts when we have closed our ears and blinded ourselves to the Father. God will speak to the ones that have allowed themselves to be pure in front of Him. He will speak and allow them to know what must be said to those asking the questions.

- Galatians 5:5 - For we, through the Spirit, wait for the hope of righteousness by faith.

The Spirit of God allows us to be enabled. Enabled is the act that can make something or someone able to achieve something. For example, we are able to move and work, day in and out, with the enabler of this being food and sleep in our lives. So, food and sleep give us the energy (enabler) for us to continue forward in our lives. The Holy Spirit in our lives enables us to follow God, wait on God, and much more.

In Galatians 5, the passage says that through the Spirit we are able to wait for the hope of righteousness, which is done by faith. And faith is gained by hearing of the word and being convicted, yet again, by the Holy Spirit in our lives. The Holy Spirit within us makes it possible, for us to have everlasting life. The Holy Spirit in us enables us to have access to our Father in Heaven. Through the Spirit of God, we are to be sanctified, given power, sealed, and much more. Without us having the Lord's Spirit in us, it would not be possible for us to have direct access to God, or for us to even be able to ask for forgiveness of our sins directly, either.

If it was not for what our Lord had done by sending and giving us the gift of the Holy Spirit, our lives would be much harder, maybe even impossible. The lives we are living today would have not been possible if not for the enabler, which is the Holy Spirit in us, opening a door for us that had been shut and that no man could open. If we as children of God allow ourselves to be enabled more and more by the Holy Spirit in our lives, we will be transformed to a point that we will look even more like our redeemer and go from glory to glory to the image of our Lord.

Holy Spirit the Caster of Demons

- Matthew 12:28 – But if I cast out devils by the Spirit of God, then the kingdom of God is come unto you.
- Luke 10:17 - And the seventy returned again with joy, saying, Lord, even the devils are subject unto us through thy name.
- Mark 9:29 - And he said unto them, This kind can come forth by nothing, but by prayer and fasting.
- Mark 9:20,25-27 - And they brought him unto him: and when he saw him, straightway the spirit tare him; and he fell on the ground, and wallowed foaming. 25. When Jesus saw that the people came running together, he rebuked the foul spirit, saying unto him, Thou dumb and deaf spirit, I charge thee, come out of him, and enter no more into him. And the spirit cried, and rent him sore, and came out of him: and he was as one dead; insomuch that many said, He is dead. But Jesus took him by the hand, and lifted him up; and he arose.

The Spirit of the Lord through us is able to cast out demons in the name of Christ. In our generation, we have many that claim to do this; I would like to let you know that many may be false or acting but the ability of casting out a demon is real and can happen with a man of God. Many will say it is not possible, but they still believe that people can be possessed - if this is the case, let me tell you now that God has fully equipped us against the Kingdom of the Devil and his forces, and His children, if they live how they need to, are equipped and can be given authority to cast out any demons in the name of Christ.

When we read the passage in Matthew 12, it says that when casting out of demons has come, the kingdom of God has also come. We need to realize that the casting out of demons is because the kingdom of God has come down for this work against the devil. We see Jesus casting out demons in Mark 9, He cast it out and raised the child back from the ground.

In addition, we see that the disciples themselves were able to cast out demons in Jesus' name and they rejoiced for it, but the Son of Man responded saying, "don't rejoice that the spirits are subject to you, but rejoice that your names are written in heaven." This is the downfall - many today have this authority given to them from God, but many will abuse it too. We need to realize there are demonic spirits (engaged in spiritual warfare) which are strong and do not just come out when you tell them to be cast out.

Jesus also responded to His disciples that some will only come out through prayer and fasting (in Mark 9:29). This is because prayer and fasting in a child of God will grow us spiritually, it will bring more anointment over us and authority to fight against the demonic forces. And this will allow you to be able to cast out demons/spirits out of people. We need to prepare ourselves, crucify the flesh, and disconnect ourselves from this world through fasting and reconnect to God in prayer.

Holy Spirit the Reminder

- John 14:26 But the Comforter, which is the Holy Ghost, whom the Father will send in my name, he shall teach you all things, and bring all things to your remembrance, whatsoever I have said unto you.

- Mark 13:11 - But when they shall lead you, and deliver you up, take no thought beforehand what ye shall speak, neither do ye premeditate: but whatsoever shall be given you in that hour, that speak ye: for it is not ye that speak, but the Holy Ghost.

In our lives, we fail many times to remember what we need to do in certain situations, but the Holy Spirit will enable us to remember. The Spirit that lives in us will cause us to remember what we must know at the point of time we need to know it. The passage in Mark 13 says that we must not worry about what we will say in certain situations because the Holy Spirit will speak for us and give us what to say in that time.

I know in my own life, in teaching, I have encountered questions that were asked of me about the Word of God, and I have seen that the Holy Spirit gave me words in my own mouth and I started speaking and answering the question. When we look at the other passage, in John 14:26, it tells us that the Holy Spirit will bring all things in remembrance to us.

Here is the thing: the word 'remember' means you must already have known it. So, for the Holy Ghost to remind you of something it means that you must have already read the Word of God and the Holy Spirit is simply reminding you of it. This is where people stumble - they assume that the Holy Spirit will tell them what to do or say, but how can He remind you of what you need if you do not know it beforehand or do not have the relationship needed so that your spiritual eyes and ears are open to hear what He is saying?

We who have the Word of God and call ourselves children of God must read the Word of God and meditate on it so

182

that when that time comes in our lives, we are ready. During whatever problem or situation you will be in, the Holy Spirit will be able to give you the proper words, for you have learned before what must be said. Now, there are times that the Holy Spirit will give you words in situations of confusion as well, this is if you have built your relationship with the Holy Spirit, just as I said above, to be able to hear in the spiritual realm what the Spirit says. But, as children of God, we must always be prepared in the Word.

Holy Spirit the one that brings Hope

- Romans 15:13 - Now the God of hope fill you with all joy and peace in believing, that ye may abound in hope, through the power of the Holy Ghost.
- Hebrews 11:1 - Now faith is the substance of things hoped for, the evidence of things not seen.
- John 6:63 - It is the spirit that quickeneth; the flesh profiteth nothing: the words that I speak unto you, they are spirit, and they are life.
- Romans 8:2 - For the law of the Spirit of life in Christ Jesus hath made me free from the law of sin and death.

Throughout our lives we do not think much about Hope. Hebrews 11 says that hope is for things that shall be, that are not seen yet. It is to cherish, to desire, and to anticipate something that is true. Hope gives joy and peace in the lives of the children of God. This hope is brought to us through the Holy Spirit.

In Romans 15, the passage says that the God of Hope will fill us with all joy and peace that we may believe, that we will abound in hope. And this hope comes from the power of the Holy Spirit.

When we read the passage in John 6, the words he speaks there are spiritual, and they are life. The Holy Spirit that dwells in us enables us to live a spirit-filled life which will also allow us to understand what we are reading in the Word of God. When we continue, in Romans 8, the passage tells us that the Spirit living life in Jesus Christ has made us free from the law, sin, and death.

When we are able to comprehend this hope, the hope we have that the Spirit of God brings, it brings an unconditional, without boundaries, hope. This hope comes because God lives inside you and me, that we may have everlasting life, that through the Holy Spirit we have a comforter, a helper, guider, and advocate. One that seals us, a revealer, praying on our behalf, speaking to us and through us.

We have such a hope for what is to come, for we know that the Holy Spirit lives in us and does so much in us and for the Kingdom of God. When we understand this in our life and know it's true, we are able to know that the hope and promises we have been given as His children, and that we have been keeping on for so long through our lives, are true; because of this the hope becomes reality.

This is a great hope and joy for the children of God, a joy and hope that keeps us going and moving forward in life. For we know and understand where we are going, towards everlasting life to be with our Lord the one that loves us, that has called us, and has given all for us, writing our names in the Book of Life.

Holy Spirit the Protector

- Acts 16:6-7 - Now when they had gone throughout Phrygia and the region of Galatia, and were forbidden of the Holy Ghost to preach the word in Asia, After they were come to Mysia, they assayed to go into Bithynia: but the Spirit suffered them not.

In our lives, the Holy Spirit is the one that can protect/guard us from the unknown spiritual or physical dangers. When we look at the passage in Acts 16, we see that it says that the Holy Spirit suffered them not to go into Bithynia and others. The word 'suffered' here means 'would not allow' them to go. You may ask, why is this? They wanted to preach the Word in Asia.

There are times we may not see everything or understand what is happening, but the Spirit will tell us or show us not to go into or enter a certain place.

Many of us, including myself, have had this experience, when you know by the Spirit not to enter a place, or go to a place, or to not do something. The reason behind this is the protection of the Holy Spirit, communicating to us not to do it, for our protection. Look at it this way: when we were younger our parents many times would communicate to us not to do something, but we still had an urge to do it. We, as humans, have a rebellious streak and ended up doing what they told us not to do. Instead of turning out how we expected it to be, that one rebellious act backfired and hurt us; instead of moving forward we moved backwards.

It is the same thing with the Holy Spirit. When the Holy Spirit communicates to us and warns us, to watch out or not to do something, we must realize that He isn't saying it for Himself or just for the fun of it. The Holy Spirit doesn't joke around - it takes the work of God seriously and when He speaks and warns us, we must listen for our own benefit and the Kingdom of God.

When we listen to the protector, the Holy Spirit, in our lives we will start realizing that it is for us, but this will also allow the kingdom of God to start growing. What I mean by this, is that when a person does not listen to the Holy Spirit's guidance and goes against it, they are no longer protected (for He protects us in the will of the Father), and instead of growing the kingdom of God, they will start tearing it apart. When we are not in the will of God it means that in that specific area and time that we were not given authority/understanding in guidance to go in that area. There are times that our Lord will send us in areas that will lead to persecution and beatings and possibly even death for your faith in Him, but this will always have an outcome that will benefit and increase the kingdom of God.

Holy Spirit the bringer of New Creation

- 2 Corinthians 5:17 - Therefore if any man be in Christ, he is a new creature: old things are passed away; behold, all things are become new.
- Colossians 3:9-10 - Lie not one to another, seeing that ye have put off the old man with his deeds; And have put on the new man, which is renewed in knowledge after the image of him that created him...
- Galatians 2:20 - I am crucified with Christ: nevertheless I live; yet not I, but Christ liveth in me: and the life which I now live in the flesh I live by the faith of the Son of God, who loved me, and gave himself for me.

When someone in the world decides to give their life to the Lord, and is sealed with the Holy Spirit, that person is a new creation in Christ. In the passage of 2 Corinthians 5, it says that if any man is in Christ this person is a new creature (creation), and anything that was in the past from the old man is gone and the new has come, which is the creation for the Holy Spirit, which has been put in you and now dwells in you.

This means that anyone that has put away the old man must also put away his deeds. These deeds are the desires of the world, before they accepted Christ, the lust and works of the flesh. He must put away those sinful actions. And what will take that empty place is the new man; this new man is not only renewed in knowledge but it's in the image of Him that created him. Showing that once we have been made new that we will start becoming as the image of Him that created us and love, patience, joy, peace, meekness, and others will start manifesting in our lives.

This happens because we have been crucified with our Lord and we no longer live, but He (Christ) lives inside you and I, through the Holy Spirit. When the Holy Spirit is in us, we have no longer the spirit of man, but the Spirit of God and we are made new. We must give glory to God that He had this love and mercy for us to give His Spirit to live in us, to make us become a new creation. This creation that allows us to have His image in us and become more like Him.

Holy Spirit the Molder/Transformer

- 2 Corinthian 3:18 - But we all, with open face beholding as in a glass the glory of the Lord, are changed into the same image from glory to glory, even as by the Spirit of the Lord.

187

- Romans 8:13-14 - For if ye live after the flesh, ye shall die: but if ye through the Spirit do mortify the deeds of the body, ye shall live. For as many as are led by the Spirit of God, they are the sons of God.
- Galatians 5:22-23 - But the fruit of the Spirit is love, joy, peace, longsuffering, gentleness, goodness, faith, meekness, temperance: against such there is no law.
- Romans 12:2 - And be not conformed to this world: but be ye transformed by the renewing of your mind, that ye may prove what is that good, and acceptable, and perfect, will of God.

In our walk with God, we need to be molded and transformed more and more in the image of Jesus Christ and go from glory to glory. You might ask yourself, why?

In the Word of God, we are told to be Holy for our Lord is Holy. That we must worship our Lord in Spirit, for He is Spirit. In Romans 8, the passage says that if we, through the power of the Spirit, put to death the deeds of our sinful nature, then we will live. When we do this, we will be able to follow the Spirit; by doing this you're led and will be the sons of God.

Bit by bit, as children of God we, through the power of the Holy Spirit, will start being molded more into the image of Christ. We will start producing the fruits of the Spirit, we will start having more love and joy and peace for others. We will start acting how our savior did with others. We, as true Christians, will not allow the world to transform us to be like them, but we will be transformed by the renewing of our minds that we may prove what is good and acceptable and the perfect will of God. We need to know and understand the reason why many of us today do not seem like Christ, or act as ambassadors of Jesus Christ, is because we are not allowing ourselves to be transformed and molded into the image of God.

When we allow ourselves to be molded more and more, when someone has done something wrong towards you, you can respond back with love and forgiveness. We will be able to understand what it means to be gentle and good towards others. In our life we will be more humble towards one another. We all have met people that call themselves Christians but even after 10+ years they do not act as Christ did and do not resemble Him in any way. Yes, we are all human, but this does not mean we cannot grow in His image as the Word of God teaches us.

A child of God that is looking to follow the will of God will always be transformed more into the image of God, for a child of God will look into his life and crucify his flesh and start seeing more how Christ is and will want to be more like Him. We would remove hatred, lies, anger, jealousy, lust, idolatry, adultery, and sexual immorality among many other desires of the flesh.

Once we realize that all of this departs us from God and allow ourselves to start removing them and being sanctified and made Holy bit by bit, we then will be called children of God for we are then truly led by the Spirit of God. The sad part is, many people believe that they don't need to clean their lives and live saying that 'God is Love.'

The Word of God also tells us He is a Just God, a Jealous God, a Righteous God; He's not just loving. This shows us that we cannot live how we want to and assume that there will not be a consequence. In Hebrews 3:12, it tells us to pay

189

attention that we don't have an evil heart of unbelief to depart from the living God. Matthew 7 shows men of God that did His will but then the Lord tells them to depart because of their acts of lawlessness, iniquity, and for being evildoers (this means someone that doesn't do God's will and follow Him). We need to start examining our life and realizing that God is calling us into holiness and living in the Spirit to be His children; you will know them for they will follow His commands.

Conclusion

As we have seen, the Holy Spirit has been given to us for much more than just the two or three subjects that many people know about. Many people today know that the Holy Spirit will convict us and the world, that we will be empowered, that we are sealed, that we will be sanctified by Him, and will be comforted by Him. As we have seen now, the Holy Spirit will also reveal to us God's will and prepare us to fulfill God's will in us for the ministry of God in many ways. The things that the Holy Spirit does, in one way or another, get dispersed through the seven-fold of the Holy Spirit, for they are separate but also one.

If the children of God started meditating on God's words and allowing themselves to truly be used by the Holy Spirit in all that has been covered up until now, the kingdom of God would prosper and grow by the Holy Spirit's works through us.

Notes

Part 7:
Rejecting the
Holy Spirit

In this chapter I would like to cover the rejection of the Holy Spirit's work in our lives. We go through our lives without thinking that we are able to grieve Him or quench Him or even lie to the Holy Spirit. There is only one sin that is not forgiven, and that is blasphemy against the Holy Spirit. I would like us to go into the Word of God and see what it reveals to us about these subjects so that we can make sure that we do not act or respond in this way towards the Holy Spirit. So we can also understand the consequences of acting this way towards the Holy Spirit and what will happen to us if we do.

Lying to the Holy Spirit

- Acts 5:1-4 - But a certain man named Ananias, with Sapphira his wife, sold a possession, And kept back part of the price, his wife also being privy to it, and brought a certain part, and laid it at the apostles' feet. But Peter said,

Ananias, why hath Satan filled thine heart to lie to the Holy Ghost, and to keep back part of the price of the land? Whiles it remained, was it not thine own? and after it was sold, was it not in thine own power? why hast thou conceived this thing in thine heart? thou hast not lied unto men, but unto God. And Ananias hearing these words fell down, and gave up the ghost: and great fear came on all them that heard these things.

Throughout our lives, we don't realize how many times we lie to God or what the consequences could be, as we see here in this passage. This passage talks about a man called Ananias and his wife by the name of Sapphira; it is said that they sold a possession that they owned, and they were planning on giving the money to God. Now, it says that they held back part of the price (money) they had from selling their possession.

The fact that they held back some of the money was not the sin in itself – but they lied to the apostles about the price they had sold their possession for. This is why, in the passage, it says, 'was not this yours, and even after you sold it, and it was in your own power (authority) to do what you wanted to do with it.' Peter says to them, "why has Satan filled your heart to lie to the Holy Spirit?" This shows that they were intentionally trying to deceive or hide the truth of what they did.

Instead of being honest to everyone, they lied about what was being done. There are times when we ourselves, instead of being honest with God with our money, emotions, friends, or family, we lie and try to deceive God and ourselves. What we don't understand is that we are not able to lie to a God that knows all. We say that we love our brother or sister or family members when, in fact, we don't.

I have met and seen many other people that will say, "this is all we can give to God" or "this is everything we can give," just as the passage shows, but it was not everything, it was only a little amount. The thing is that many times these people give out that information even without being asked if they had more. In fact, they respond only to show that what they are doing, what they have, comes from a heart that is filled with pride, and a deceitful heart to prove to others what is going on.

When doing the work of God, we must understand that God is present, He is there, He is watching everything. We need to watch what we speak and make sure that what we speak is honest and we live in integrity. In the situation from the passage above, deceit brought death to Ananias and Saphira. In our life, it can lead to death in the physical and also in the spiritual life. We need to make sure that we are representing Christ in our life, in our actions, and in our words – being honest not deceitful.

Grieving the Holy Spirit

• Ephesians 4:30 - And grieve not the holy Spirit of God, whereby ye are sealed unto the day of redemption.

We are capable in our lives, through actions or through our language, to grieve the Holy Spirit. Grieving someone means causing anguish or mourning over what is done. This grieving comes from us displeasing our Father in heaven through our walk with God, when our life does not show us as true ambassadors, not identifying our life with how Christ's was. This indicates that our life is not a holy walk, but a walk in the impure, walking away from God.

The way our generation lives today, disobeying the Word of God but saying that they are children of God, is because our generation has twisted the Word of God, believing that what is good is evil and what is evil is good. They do not want to take and accept conviction in their hearts. This has caused many today that are children of God to be confused and to disobey the voice of the Holy Spirit in their lives. When the Holy Spirit tells you to stand up or to listen, or when He convicts you of something that is wrong in your life or of other things and you don't listen, this will grieve the Holy Spirit. The Holy Spirit will mourn, because He desires to fulfill the will of God, and you have denied the will of God.

When we do not listen or obey the will of God in our life, when we hear the voice of God speaking to us and we do not listen, this will grieve the Holy Spirit. For the Holy Spirit knows the will of God is the perfect will and perfect path for you. When we don't listen to the Holy Spirit, He will mourn for He will know that by not listening or obeying the will of God we will depart from God. When He guides us to truth, and our disobeying instead leads us further away from God and the truth, He mourns for us. He knows that one day will come, if you continue disobeying and going in the wrong direction, that you will depart from the living God due to your own evil heart of unbelief in God's plan, purpose, will, and guidance in your life.

Quenching the Holy Spirit
- 1 Thessalonians 5:19 - Quench not the Spirit.

When we contemplate the word "quenching," we think about putting something out, like extinguishing a fire. When we hear someone say that they are thirsty, we tell them to "quench their thirst;" what this means is to drink something so you can extinguish or put out you thirst, for you to no longer be thirsty.

This is the same thing that this verse is talking about. It is telling us not to quench the Spirit in doing the will of God. The Holy Spirit desires, craves, to fulfill the will of the Father in your life.

In the passage above, when we read the context, it tells us to be patient, comfort the feebleminded, support the weak, not to pay evil for evil, and that we must follow that which is good. It continues further, telling us to rejoice and pray without ceasing among others. When you and I do not follow what God tell us to do in His commands, statues, or laws, we start quenching the Spirit in us. When we start quenching the Spirit, which is power (Fire), in us that is burning to do the will of God, it becomes weaker in us and smaller. This is not saying that the Holy Spirit is weaker, but because you are not using what was given to you, it starts quenching the Spirit which wants to do the will of God in your life.

The dangerous thing about quenching the Spirit is that when we quench something to its limit, we can also put it out completely. This shows us that if we eventually stop allowing the Holy Spirit to work, we become numb to it. If we allow it to, it will quench to a point that we will no longer feel it for we ourselves have left the Spirit of God behind.

The Word of God tells us that He will never forsake us. This is true, but we ourselves are able to forsake Him and leave Him behind to a point of losing our salvation. We must stay alert and not allow ourselves to become numb to the Spirit of God.

Resisting the Holy Spirit

- Acts 7:51 - Ye stiff necked and uncircumcised in heart and ears, ye do always resist the Holy Ghost: as your fathers did, so do ye.

I included resisting the Holy Spirit here towards the end after grieving, lying, and quenching the Holy Spirit. The reason behind this is because resisting the Holy Spirit is what leads us to these other three. To resist is to withstand something, to not allow it to influence us in a situation or problem in our lives. As we know, the Holy Spirit is the one to guide and lead us into the will of the Father. The Holy Spirit is what actually influences us to action in our life.

We, as children of God, should not resist or withstand the Holy Spirit's influence in our lives, but we should accept it and surrender all to Him for us to follow the will of God. If God has been pulling you into the direction of preaching the Word of God or to give Him praise through music, or to speak to someone at work/school/store we must not resist but follow. When we allow Him to influence us in the path of righteousness and holiness, we will fulfill the will of God.

When we comprehend this, we realize that if the Holy Spirit is what pulls us to an action, the action of the will of God, then we must follow it. If we resist to do what the Holy Spirit is telling us, which will always work with the Word of God, then it will lead us to quench the Holy Spirit and its work, which will lead Him to grieve for us for we are departing willingly from doing the will of God. This eventually will lead us to lie because we have become numb to the Holy Spirit's influence and guidance in our lives. We need to become more aware and

201

surrender all to the Holy Spirit, for us not to fall away but to stay strong in the will of the Father.

Blasphemy against the Holy Spirit

- Mark 3:22-30 - And the scribes which came down from Jerusalem said, He hath Beelzebub, and by the prince of the devils casteth he out devils. And he called them unto him, and said unto them in parables, How can Satan cast out Satan? And if a kingdom be divided against itself, that kingdom cannot stand. And if a house be divided against itself, that house cannot stand. And if Satan rise up against himself, and be divided, he cannot stand, but hath an end. No man can enter into a strong man's house, and spoil his goods, except he will first bind the strong man; and then he will spoil his house. Verily I say unto you, All sins shall be forgiven unto the sons of men, and blasphemies wherewith soever they shall blaspheme: But he that shall blaspheme against the Holy Ghost hath never forgiveness, but is in danger of eternal damnation. Because they said, He hath an unclean spirit.

The word 'blasphemy' is an action or transgression of talking irreverently about God. The passage above speaks about how the scribes said that Jesus was removing devils with devils. The passage makes it sound broad or vague, and this is why people are confused about this. We need to understand that just because something is broad doesn't mean that it doesn't makes sense or have specific purpose. The reason it is broad here is because that is the definition of 'blasphemy' against the Holy Spirit. The definition explains it as taking an action against or talking about what is considered holy and the work of holiness and to say that it isn't or using what is considered holy and taking it out of context or being disrespectful towards it.

As we see in the passage above, blasphemy was dedicating what was holy and true in front of God through the work of the Holy Spirit and saying it was devil's work. This is taking what is holy and saying it is not and that the work of the Holy Spirit is not His. When someone is truly speaking through the Holy Spirit, or prophesying, healing, doing miracles, having visions or dreams, and someone attributes this to the devil, this is blasphemy against the Holy Spirit, for this which is holy and the work of the Holy Spirit you cannot dedicate to something else. We must examine all things and make sure it is with the Word of God.

This is why we must be very measured in speaking against what we see in the house of God. When the Holy Spirit is speaking we must process, examine, and ask God to reveal it to us. The problem about the passage above is that the scribes didn't listen, they didn't process, and didn't have the patience for what was happening; instead of examining what was going on they spoke against what was happening. This came from their own ignorance and pride of thinking they knew everything, a place of not wanting to lose their position, and afraid to admit that what was going on was from God. For if they admitted it, they might have been embarrassed or even scared that they might have to fight against the devil himself and his army.

We must be aware of what is going on, we must understand the Word of God. We need to be slow to speak against what we see to make sure we do not commit the sin that cannot be forgiven. I would like to say that if you are able to accept Christ as your Lord then you can also let Him go. Many people believe that blasphemy cannot be committed by a child of God, for if he is saved, he is always saved. This teaching of always saved or that children of God cannot blasphemy is not in the Word of God.

As you've seen throughout this book, there are multiple passages that show that someone that is saved can also lose his salvation if he departs from God. We need to understand, first of all, that someone that doesn't follow God or know God wouldn't know about the Holy Spirit and he can't blasphemy against something he does not know. What we need to realize is that only someone that knows God and is a child of God, would know what type of works are attributed to the Holy Spirit and because of this, they will know what type of work the Holy Spirit does. This means that these verses that are written are spoken to the children of God; that they must not blasphemy and that we must stay strong and not become numb to the Holy Spirit so as to not commit this act against the Holy Spirit.

Notes

Conclusion

I first would like to say all the glory goes to God our Lord for without Him and His mercy and grace that He has given me, I would not have been able to do any of this. The wisdom and knowledge was from Him, He gave me counsel through the Holy Spirit to understand. I pray that all of you will begin to have the true Spirit of Fear in you, of reverence for our God, to start allowing yourself to grow mightier in Him through His Great Spirit.

Furthermore, I hope that all will start growing in the Holy Spirit, to be filled in the Holy Spirit and eventually be baptized in the Holy Spirit, the Gift of God. So we can allow God's magnificent power to be shown and His Kingdom to grow. Remember that our Lord is watching all, He is observing all with His great, divine insight. This can be either for your reward or damnation.

The Holy Spirit can do so much for you and me; it is time to allow the Spirit of God to start truly working in our lives. If you allow Him, He can give you wisdom and much more, He can reveal to you all things. The Spirit can truly be your comforter and helper. Overall, He can teach you and show you all things. It is time to depend on Him in your life more and more so He can start working in your life to fullest extent, what God had planned before you were even born.

Thank you for reading Deciphering the Holy Ghost, taking the time to do so. Every moment that we use to study our Father and what He has given you and I makes a difference. When we can understand why the Holy Spirit was given to us and what He can accomplish through us if we allow Him, we then allow our Father's will in us to be fulfilled.

Glory to God,

God Bless You

David Muresan